# The Custer Fight
# and
# Other Tales of the Old West

### Larry D. Underwood

**Media Publishing**
Lincoln, Nebraska

Library of Congress #88-62108
ISBN 0-939644-40-1

Portions of the following stories have previously been published:
"Marcus A. Reno: Reno's Luck" and "Reno's Early Life" in *Illinois*
magazine (1979); "Charles A. Reynolds: The Death of Lonesome
Charley" in *True West* (1985); "Comanche: The Survivor" in *Canada
Rides* (1974); "Rowdy Joe Lowe" in *Illinois* (1980); "The Earps" in
*Illinois* (1977); "The Day Hickok Died" in *Outdoor Illinois* (1973);
"Allan Pinkerton and the West" in *True West* (1984); "Black Bart,
PO8" in *Illinois* (1983).

Cover design by Tony Schappaugh
Text design by C.J. Westrick

**MEDIA PUBLISHING**
(Div. of M.P.M., Inc.)
2440 'O' Street, Suite 202
Lincoln, Nebraska 68510-1125

*Dedicated to*
*my history teachers:*
*Elaine Hood*
*Charles W. Smith*
*Glenn Huron Seymour, Ph.D.*
*D. Alexander Brown*

# Table of Contents

# Foreword

During the quarter of a century I've known Larry Underwood, he has amazed me with his unwavering enthusiasm for the Old West and its remarkable characters. He is constantly digging for new information that he is eager to pass along to his friends and readers. He is the sort of enthusiast who will call you up in the middle of the night to share with you some beguiling anecdote his searches have turned up.

When I first met Larry he was teaching school near the Illinois bank of the Mississippi, and I visualized him as spending his recreational hours peering across the river to probe the farthest reaches of the Old West. He was writing a series of articles about people from Illinois who had ventured into the West during the 19th century and made names for themselves of almost legendary proportions. He tracked a considerable number of these adventurers and spent many hours of pure scholarly research so as to tell their stories in the right way. He is one researcher who never stints on his time to get the facts.

Now, in this new work, he has aplied his skills to various characters who have attracted his interest during years of study of the Western frontier. There are well-known names like Custer, Reno, Sitting Bull, the Earp brothers, and the outlaw rhymester Black Bart. Just as intriguing are the sketches of lesser known characters such as Lonesome Charley Reynolds, Rowdy Joe Lowe, and Old Bill Miner. Larry writes in the manner he uses when telling a friend about these people face to face or on the telephone. He has given them all a fresh and lively treatment. There is not a dull page in this book, which proves that what truly fascinates a meticulous researcher and writer is bound to have the same effect upon his readers.

**Dee Alexander Brown**
Author, *Bury My Heart at Wounded Knee*

# Introduction

In 1876, the Great American West was still a remote, unknown land for most of America's forty million citizens. And even though the nation celebrated its one-hundredth birthday that year, and even though mountain men, explorers, settlers, soldiers and fortune hunters had swept over the vast sea of Plains grass and into the Rocky Mountains, the West was still largely a frontier society.

The West was still a crude land protected by military posts and camps, seventy-six of them by an 1874 count, that scattered 17,819 commissioned officers and enlisted men (eight cavalry regiments and seventeen infantry regiments) over more than a million square miles of frontier country.

In the East, where things were more settled, fireworks, bands, bells and city officials in Philadelphia kicked off America's 1876 birthday party on January 1.

An act to appropriate money for the Centennial celebration passed the U.S. House of Representatives on January 25 and the U.S. Senate two weeks later. President Ulysses S. Grant quickly signed it into law using an eagle quill from one of America's birds that someone had shot.

In the meantime, William A. Hulbert and others, on February 2, met in New York City's Grand Central Hotel and created pro baseball's National League. And on February 14, Alexander Graham Bell patented his telephone.

In 1876, there was a Democrat majority in the House. And since 1876 was a Presidential election year, those Democrats were concerned with Republican antics of the past decade and a half. Eagerly, they were checking into any improprieties.

One matter that concerned the Democrats was the great sums of money being given to President Grant's private secretary, Orville Babcock. Whiskey distilleries, first in St. Louis, then in Peoria, Milwaukee and Chicago, paid bribes more willingly than taxes. By so doing, they saved an estimated million dollars or more annually.

Babcock was tried in St. Louis for his role in the Whiskey Ring and a controversial jury freed him after hearing pleas from the President. Later, on the day of Babcock's victory over justice, St. Louis friends, the story goes, slipped him $10,000 for his trouble and he returned to Washington, D.C. President Grant had seen enough; the President let Babcock go a few days later.

In March, Secretary of War William W. Belknap was charged in a scandal called the Indian Ring. Belknap, according to his accusers, sold a War Department post-tradership on the military post at Fort Sill. This appointment was a normal function of the political spoils system, but the money had soiled the deal. Belknap resigned, was impeached anyhow, and acquitted in July.

But most Americans were watching other occurrences in 1876. Some marveled that Rose Harland and Nell Sanders slugged it out in the United States' first public boxing match between women. That was on March 16. And at 9 a.m. on May 10 at Philadelphia's Fairmount Park, the Centennial Exhibition officially opened. President Grant and other dignitaries were on the podium when Susan B. Anthony and four women charged the stage and presented a declaration of women's rights, disrupting the ceremonies.

And from June 1 to June 4, passengers clung to the *Lightning Train* that crossed the United States from New York City to San Francisco in a blazing 83 hours and 39 minutes.

The Republicans collected in Cincinnati to nominate their Presidential candidate Rutherford B. Hayes in early June, and in late June the Democrats selected a bachelor, Samuel J. Tilden, in St. Louis.

Fifty thousand people sweltered in the 90°F heat in Philadelphia's Independence Square on July 4 to celebrate the birthday of the land of freedom, justice and equal opportunity. A few days later, in Hamburg, South Carolina, decades of hatred, ignorance and prejudice exploded into shooting. Black and white deaths stained the nation's birthday with what is known as the Hamburg Massacre.

And on August 1, Colorado became a state—the 38th. In Savannah, Georgia, between August and November, 940 residents died during a Yellow Fever outbreak.

In the meantime, in Menlo Park, New Jersey, during September, Thomas Edison opened a laboratory and on November 7, Democrat Samuel Tilden won the Presidential election. Well, not really. The majority of American voters wanted him and chose him, but the electoral college majority did not favor Tilden. (Hayes was finally declared a winner by a panel of eight Republicans and seven Democrats in March 1877 after a deal was struck with Democrats.)

That same night, November 7, Terrence Mullin and Jack Hughes tried to slip into President Abraham Lincoln's tomb and steal the body from its Springfield, Illinois resting place. Mullin and Hughes failed.

So in a year when all this was happening in the East, where more settled, civilized Americans lived, there was also a frontier society in the western United States where events occurred that helped shape the nation.

But in the West there were people that belonged to a different age. They were the Plains Indians. And there were the people who populated the frontier. They were the soldiers and frontiersmen. And the Plains Indians were on a collision course with the soldiers and frontiersmen. For them, 1876 would also be a year to remember.

# Part I

# The Custer Fight

# The Battle of the Little Bighorn

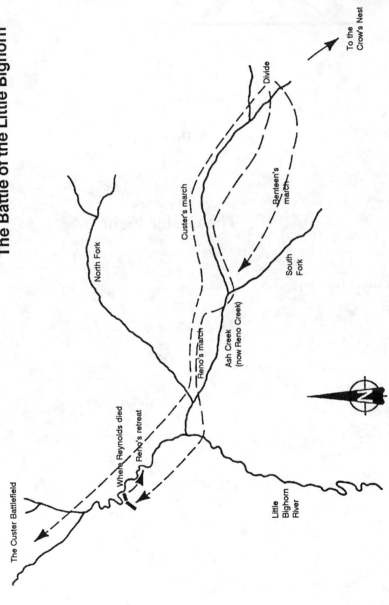

# 1      The Custer Fight

In 1876, a three-pronged assault by the U.S. Army on Sioux and Cheyenne Indians in Montana led to a June 25 showdown on the Little Bighorn River. A regiment of cavalry, the U.S. Seventh Cavalry, commanded by Lieutenant Colonel George Armstrong Custer found the Indian camp that Sunday. Custer divided his command and sent three companies under Major Marcus Reno to attack one end of the village while Custer and five companies rode to attack the other end.

Custer and his detachment were completely wiped out, while Reno saved some of his men by retreating to high ground and defending against his attackers until Colonel John Gibbon and General Alfred Terry arrived on June 27.

Serving as Chief of Scouts for George A. Custer on June 25, 1876, was Charley Reynolds. He was ordered to accompany Major Reno's command. When the attack turned into a retreat, Reynolds died bravely, protecting his fleeing comrades.

In the huge Indian camp was the Hunkpapa Sioux medicine man Sitting Bull. Too old and too important to fight, he observed the battle, then over the next months traveled with his people to Canada and safety. His return to the United States and subsequent death marked the end of the era of the Plains Indians.

But there were other heroes of the battle. One of the most celebrated survivors was a cavalry horse named Comanche. He and other horses who survived the Custer Fight were often honored and held in high esteem by those who later owned them.

All of these—soldiers, Indians, scouts and horses—are a part of the great mystique that has grown up around the Custer Fight.

# 2    George Armstrong Custer: The Last Stand

The smell of blood and death was everywhere. The hot sun glared and in the distance summer heat billowed off the ridges, dancing and rippling. Great brown mounds, dead horses, lay bloated, swollen and stinking. Their huge eyes stared blankly, mouths open, tongues dangling.

Men's naked bodies lay slashed and dirty, swollen, discolored, chopped and cut up. Their blood-encrusted flesh was pale with the alkaline dust that had settled over everything. Here and there birds scavenged and millions of flies buzzed and crawled over the decaying men and horses.

Abdomens cut open, intestines sometimes in place, often not, decayed now in the hot sun. Feet, hands, legs and arms crudely severed, lay scattered about. Now and then a body had no head.

Here and there, a cluster of feathered arrows stood up out of the clumps of gray-green sagebrush, marking another rotting body.

Moving north toward the crest of the ridge, a breastwork of dead horses lay ringing an area about thirty yards square. More than thirty horses and over forty dead men lay bunched in this deadly square.

And just there amid the carnage, a naked, pale-skinned man with blondish-red hair sat up, leaning slightly backward against two naked, dead men, one across the other. His upper right arm was laying on the topmost body. His right forearm and hand supported his head. He wore only socks.

On closer inspection, a trickle of dried blood was on his left chest and side. The blood had oozed from a bullet hole just beneath the heart. It was a fatal wound. Another in the right forearm was not much. The face was not anguished, but rather looked as if he were only resting. The light-colored hair was thinning and cut short. In the left temple, there was another bullet hole, a clean wound, no blood.

It was June 26, 1876. Less than twenty-four hours earlier, this man, Lieutenant Colonel George Armstrong Custer, charged to the top of this hill and died. With him, over two hundred soldiers of the U.S. Seventh Cavalry died also.

This was Custer's Last Stand, but where did Custer begin?

George Armstrong Custer began in New Rumley, Ohio, just west of Steubenville, on December 5, 1839. A tiny farming community, New Rumley was laid out twenty-seven years earlier by George's great uncle, Jacob Custer.

Of German descent, George's father, Emmanuel, was born at Cresaptown, Maryland. After his wife, Matilda Viers, died in 1835 leaving him with three children, the part-time farmer and blacksmith married Maria Kirkpatrick, a widow with two children. Together, Emmanuel and Maria (of Scotch-Irish descent) had seven children. The first two died in infancy and then came George. He was followed by Nevin J. (an invalid), Thomas Ward, Boston and Margaret.

Young George attended the McNeely Normal School at Hopedale, about eight miles from New Rumley. He was apprenticed to a cabinetmaker in Cadiz, the county seat of his native Harrison County, but in 1849 he moved to Monroe City, Michigan (population 3,500) to live with his half-sister and her husband, Lydia and David Reed. He attended Alfred Stebins' Young Men's Academy there in Monroe on Lake Erie and was an excellent student, graduating when he was sixteen years old.

The young graduate returned to Harrison County, Ohio and taught school at Locust Grove and later, near Athens, at Beech Point. That same year, 1856, he wrote for a United States Military Academy appointment. Congressman John A. Bingham had none left, but told young George to write next year. In 1857, he tried again and was accepted. One hundred eight candidates began testing on June 20; sixty-eight were accepted. George Armstrong Custer of Ohio was one of them.

When classes began in 1857, Custer expected to graduate in 1862. The course lasted five years at that time. Custer's West Point career was remarkable — but in the negative. He accrued demerits like few others, getting nearly 200 demerits in some years. Interestingly, his totals always fell just short of expulsion.

In 1861 with the first shots of the Civil War, the Classes of 1861 and 1862 petitioned the Secretary of War for early graduation. Permission was granted and May 6, 1861 was graduation day for the Class of 1861; June 24, 1861 was graduation day for Custer and the Class of 1862. Of the sixty-eight admitted in 1857, twenty-two quit to join the Confederate Army. Others had dropped out or were dismissed over the years, and only thirty-four remained. Custer graduated last in his class.

Less than a week later a fight broke out at West Point. Custer's duty was to stop it. He didn't and was arrested and jailed. At his July 15 court-martial, he was only reprimanded, then ordered to Washington, D.C. and assigned to Company G, Major Innes Palmer's Second Cavalry, General Irvin McDowell's command, in time to lead a charge at the First Battle of Bull Run. Congressman Bingham, who had appointed Custer to West Point wrote, "Young Custer sprang to the front — and was a hero."

In 1862, Custer was appointed to General George Brinton McClellan's staff and breveted for "gallant, brave, meritorious service" for Gettysburg (summer 1863), Yellow Tavern (May 1864), Winchester (September 1864), Fisher's Hill (September 1864), and Five Forks (Spring 1865).

Custer served Brigadier General Alfred Pleasonton as an aide beginning in early spring, 1863. In June, Custer was promoted to Brigadier General when Pleasonton shook up his command to put a stop to Confederate Cavalry General J.E.B. Stuart's harassing tactics. Custer took command of the Second Michigan Brigade of the Third Cavalry, General Hugh Judson Kilpatrick's Division.

Just over a year later, in October 1864, Custer took command of the Third Cavalry Division, Army of the Potomac, one of General Philip Sheridan's three divisions. He was promoted to Major General of U.S. Volunteers on April 15, 1865. He was just twenty-five years old and his division had stopped Confederate General Robert E. Lee's retreat to help in the surrender which ended the war. May 23,

1865 found Custer riding down Pennsylvania Avenue in Washington, D.C. in the Grand Review of the Army of the Potomac, wondering where he'd go from here.

In November 1862, while on leave to Monroe, Michigan, he'd formally met Judge Daniel Stanton Bacon's daughter, Elizabeth Clift Bacon. Elizabeth, or Libbie, was the only survivor of four children of Judge Bacon and an 1862 graduate of Boyd's Seminary. And in late September 1863, he took a 25-day leave to Michigan and was back at Monroe on Tuesday, February 9, 1864. Just after 6 p.m., Custer and Libbie were married at the First Presbyterian Church by Reverend Erasmus J. Boyd, assisted by Reverend D.C. Mattoon. Of her husband, Libbie wrote later, "Yet without the least intention, I captured the greatest prize of all."

The happy couple rode a train east to West Point, then to New York City and Washington, D.C. Their new "home" was Custer's winter headquarters, a farm house, five miles south of Brandy Station, Virginia.

Now with the War over in 1865, General Philip Sheridan assigned Custer to accompany him to Texas. Confederate General Edmund Kirby Smith had not yet surrendered, but before Custer arrived Smith surrendered and so the mission became an excuse to occupy Texas and show the French the United States' disappointment at their presence in Mexico.

Custer and Libbie rode steamboats down the Ohio and Mississippi rivers to New Orleans, then up the Red River, eventually riding cross-country to the vicinity of Austin and San Antonio, Texas. Custer had arrived in the West.

Still a major general, Custer was earning $8,000 per year. Sheridan recommended he be given that rank permanently, but politics probably kept that from happening. Custer was a Democrat and did not hold enough animosity toward the South for the Radical Republicans who held power.

In January 1866, Custer's volunteer commission expired. Suddenly, he was a captain in the Regular Army, Fifth U.S. Cavalry, making $2,000 per year. He asked for leave and traveled by boat from Galveston to New Orleans, then north to Monroe, Michigan.

Over the coming months, he sought work. He was offered a commission as Major General of Caballeros by Porfirio Díaz and Benito Juárez of Mexico. They were anxious to oust the Frenchman Maximilian. He was offered a great deal of money—some say $16,000, others $10,000—for a year's work, but U.S. President Andrew Johnson refused him permission.

Custer applied for the new position of Inspector General of United States Cavalry and was refused. Finally on July 28, 1866, he was given the rank of Lieutenant Colonel. He was assigned to be second-in-command of the newly created U.S. Seventh Cavalry, a unit whose mission was to deal with Plains Indians.

Custer had given some thought to entering politics. In August and September, he and Libbie accompanied President Andrew Johnson on a political swing through the country where the President hoped to rally votes for those opposed to the Radical Republicans in the Congressional elections in the fall of 1866. General U.S. Grant was along. Everywhere, to their embarrassment, they suffered anti-Johnson sentiment.

And so, with any political hopes dormant for the time being, Custer and Libbie caught a train for Fort Riley, Kansas. His commander was Colonel Andrew Jackson Smith. The Seventh's duty was to protect railroad construction crews speeding across America to tie the East with California and particularly deal with those Indians along the Republican and Smoky Hill rivers.

In December 1866, when Captain William Judd Fetterman rode out of Fort Phil Kearny and into the history books, a shock wave rippled from that tiny Wyoming outpost to Washington, D.C. Fetterman's distinction: He lost his entire command of eighty men to Indians in what the Army and government of the United States call the Fetterman Massacre. Government and Army reaction pretty well influenced Indian policy to the time that Custer, leading more men, met a similar fate and relegated Fetterman's mistake to only second worst.

General Winfield Scott Hancock, commanding the Department of Missouri, Division of Missouri, organized a spring 1867 expedition against Cheyenne, Sioux and Arapahoe tribes in which Custer and the

*General Custer as he looked at the end of the Civil War. This uniform was of his design, complete with scarf and collar. (Courtesy of the National Archives.)*

Seventh participated. Nothing much came of the campaign. A few skirmishes, none significant, left an occasional band without food or clothing, some killed or wounded, and all enraged. The Indians, in turn, took out their bitterness on white settlers or unfortunate travelers.

During the Hancock expedition, about 1,400 infantry, artillery and cavalry soldiers traced Smoky Hill stage road to Fort Harker, four miles from present Ellsworth, Kansas, and then south to the Santa Fe Trail along the Arkansas River. Hancock established a headquarters at Fort Larned, not far from present Larned, Kansas.

When a band of Cheyenne fled north, Custer was sent after them. Nothing much came of the chase except that while trying to kill his first buffalo, Custer's horse threw up his head and caught a pistol shot between the ears, leaving Custer horseless and alone on the Plains. And while chasing around under the blistering sun in relentless Great

Plains winds, several of his troopers deserted. Custer's orders: "Stop those men. Shoot them where you find them. Don't bring in any alive." And three men were wounded; one died later.

Just over a week later in miserable Kansas heat, Custer force-marched his men 150 miles in sixty hours. The trip was from Fort Wallace to Fort Hays. Then without orders, he raced off to Fort Harker, where, without permission, he grabbed a ride on the Kansas Pacific, headed for Fort Riley and his Libbie. On the Fort Harker march, two of his men, exhausted and suffering from the heat, fell behind and were killed by Indians.

Ten days later, Custer was arrested and charged with leaving his command, shooting deserters, abandoning the two men killed by Indians, and marching his troops for too long a period. There were three other charges, including damaging government horses. The court-martial that followed convicted him and his punishment was "to be suspended from rank and command for one year, and to forfeit his pay proper for the same time." The sentence became effective on November 20, 1867, and the Custer's spent the winter at Fort Leavenworth with the soon-to-be commander of the Department of Missouri, General Philip Sheridan, Custer's Civil War commander and friend. In June 1868, the Custers returned to Monroe and remained there until Sheridan sent for them.

Sheridan was determined to solve the Indian problem. He formulated a plan whereby a three-pronged campaign would converge on the Canadian and Washita river valleys in western Indian Territory— now Oklahoma—and catch the Indians in their winter camps when their women, old men and children would not be easily moved.

According to Sheridan's plan, a column commanded by Major Andrew W. Evans would move east from Fort Bascom (near present Logan, New Mexico), another commanded by Major Eugene A. Carr would ride southeast from Fort Lyon (near present La Junta, Colorado), and another commanded by Lieutenant Colonel Alfred Sully would make its way south from Fort Dodge (five miles east of present Dodge City, Kansas).

Custer had served nearly ten months of his suspension by late September 1868 and Sheridan, General William Tecumseh Sherman and

Lieutenant Colonel Sully all wanted Custer on active duty. So Sheridan telegraphed Custer to return to Kansas. Sheridan wanted him to lead the Seventh Cavalry in the Fort Dodge column.

In early November, the winterized Seventh Cavalry, five companies of infantry, a 450-wagon train and the Nineteenth Kansas Volunteer Cavalry, Colonel Samuel J. Crawford commanding, moved south to establish Camp Supply (15 miles northwest of present Woodward, Oklahoma). Lieutenant Colonel Alfred Sully was in command of the Fort Dodge column, but when Sheridan joined the forces at Camp Supply he ordered Sully back to headquarters and put Custer in command.

Sheridan also brought word of an Indian trail he'd spotted and ordered Custer to go after the Indians immediately. At 3 a.m. November 23, Custer was up to prepare for the march south. Snow was falling and piling up fast. Sheridan asked Custer, "What do you think?"

Looking into the blowing snow, already a foot deep, Custer nodded, "It's all right. We can move. The Indians can't."

At 6 a.m., dressed in fur hats and long overcoats, the Seventh Cavalry, complete with regimental band, plodded off through the heavy snow. They continued south in bitter cold until, on Thanksgiving Day, November 26, Major Joel H. Elliott, scouting the Canadian River, found a trail and sent word to Custer.

Custer ordered Elliott to follow the trail until 8 p.m., then wait. At 9 p.m., Custer and the Seventh found Elliott. They rested for an hour during which time the Seventh boiled coffee and ate hardtack. After an hour, with the moon up, they marched off to find the Indian camp.

Before long, scouts discovered dying embers from small fires, probably started earlier by boys guarding a pony herd. The herd and boys had gone, but the village had to be close by. Soon, at the crest of a hill, they spied the little village down on the Washita River. There were fifty-one lodges (47 Cheyenne, 2 Arapahoe, and 2 Sioux).

Custer split his command with orders to strike at dawn from four sides. Quietly, they took their positions and waited.

By first light, a heavy fog shrouded the valley and Indian camp. Custer's soldiers moved like ghosts in the fog, their horses' hooves muffled by the snow.

Suddenly, there was a gunshot in the village. Custer screamed for the band to play and the madness of the attack began. The band blared the "Garry Owen" and a mix of gunfire, women and children screaming, men cheering and war whooping rattled around in the midst of it all. It took only ten minutes to take the village, but the fighting continued off and on the remainder of the day, as bands of Indians from neighboring camps occasionally appeared and were repulsed by Custer's outer defense.

In the meantime, the soldiers, according to Custer's report, were destroying 1,100 buffalo robes, 700 pounds of tobacco, 4,000 arrows, 500 pounds of powder, 1,000 pounds of lead and tons of dried meat. Custer also reported destroying 875 Indian ponies. His men burned some of the goods and threw the rest in the river.

During the fight, Major Elliott, who'd commanded the Seventh while Custer was suspended, took a detachment of about fifteen men and chased after a band of Indians who'd shown themselves on a nearby hill. As Elliott rode out of sight, there was gunfire, and through the rest of the day, no sign of Elliott. Toward dark, with other Indian camps threatening, Custer formed up the Seventh, ordered the band to play and marched directly toward the Indians. When the Indians scattered, Custer wheeled and marched north toward Camp Supply, leaving Major Elliott and his men to their fate.

Custer put the Indian's losses at 105 warriors killed. (Since it was such a small village, later counts claim this was more than likely only thirty-eight.) He claimed to have captured fifty-three women and children. At the village, he lost one officer, Captain Louis Hamilton, and had eleven enlisted men and three officers, including his brother Tom Custer, wounded.

Thomas Ward Custer, born in 1845, had been with his brother since November 1864 when he joined General Custer's staff as a lieutenant. Tom made captain on February 11, 1865 and was breveted colonel for bravery in April 1865. He'd won two Congressional Medals of Honor and was commissioned into the Regular Army after the war, rejoining his brother's regiment in July 1866.

Still missing were Major Elliott and his detachment. (Their dead and mutilated bodies were found on December 11. They lay two miles from the Washita battlefield.) On arrival at Camp Supply, Custer's victorious Seventh marched in review. Indian scouts chanted victory songs and the buckskin-clad white scouts and the mounted Indian prisoners made quite a sight. Despite the December cold, the regimental band was again bravely playing the "Garry Owen."

Even though the Washita fight has often been called a massacre, it was indeed a big victory for the Army. They'd tried since 1865 to count a victory over the Plains Indians. Now they had it and Custer had done it. He received congratulations from General William T. Sherman and Secretary of War John M. Schofield.

Operations continued in the area until the spring of 1869 when Custer and the Seventh were ordered to Fort Hays. The Southern Plains Indians were considered under control with the exception of a band led by Tall Bull and he'd moved his people north.

Custer was never the full commander of the Seventh, but the commander never seemed to be around during these years. Custer kept busy when not in the field by writing magazine articles for publications like *Turf, Field and Farm* and *Forest and Stream*. That summer of 1869 Custer applied for the position of Commandant of the U.S. Military Academy at West Point. He didn't get it and that December was on leave in Michigan.

Following another summer at Fort Hays, Custer decided to take leave in the winter of 1870–71 to look for other employment. He hoped for a better paying job and divided his time between Michigan and New York City, but found nothing suitable.

Back on duty, in September 1871, Custer was ordered forty or so miles south of Louisville, Kentucky to Elizabethtown where he and the Seventh had orders to suppress the Ku Klux Klan and enforce federal tax laws on distilleries. Custer, however, spent much of his time traveling through the South inspecting government horse purchases. In his spare time, he wrote a history of the Hancock campaign of 1867 for *Galaxy* magazine.

In January 1872, General Sheridan ordered Custer to accompany the 19-year-old son of Czar Alexander II of Russia on a Great Plains hunting trip. About five years earlier, the Russians had sold Alaska to the United States. This hunting trip was considered a good-will gesture toward the Russians. On their return from the Plains, the Grand Duke Alexis traveled to Louisville. He invited Custer and Libbie to accompany his party on a steamboat to New Orleans.

The Custers made the trip and returned to Monroe, Michigan, by March 7, 1872, for George's sister Margaret's wedding to Lieutenant James Calhoun of the Seventh. The Custers then returned to Elizabethtown, Kentucky, for the remainder of 1872.

In February 1873, the Seventh was ordered to Dakota Territory. They were to guard the surveyors for the Northern Pacific Railroad as they sought a rail route through Montana. In the last week of March, the Seventh assembled at Memphis, Tennessee and rode steamboats to Cairo, Illinois where they boarded trains for Yankton, Dakota Territory.

The Seventh marched the 353 miles from Yankton to Fort Rice, twenty-five miles below Bismarck, by June 10. They trained for ten days and then joined the Yellowstone Expedition commanded by Colonel David S. Stanley. The column contained 1,451 men, 79 officers, 275 wagons and 700 beef cattle.

From the beginning, Custer and Stanley did not get along. Custer was reprimanded. He left the column without permission. Then Stanley arrested him and made him take the Seventh to the end of the column. They met the steamer *Far West* at the mouth of Glendive Creek and an engineer for the railroad insisted Custer be released and the Seventh be placed at the head of the column.

By July 31, the expedition was camped north of the mouth of the Powder River. The Seventh continued up the Yellowstone River, arriving across from the Tongue River on August 4 where they came under fire from Indians on the south side of the Yellowstone. Two men, veterinarian John Holzinger and a sutler, were caught away from the regiment and slain. On August 9, there was more trouble and Custer tried to chase Indians who'd crossed the Yellowstone, but the Army horses balked at swimming the river. On August 11, he skirmished with the Indians again and had casualties of one killed and three wounded. Thus ended Custer's first action against the Indians of the northern Plains.

*General Philip Sheridan, Custer's friend and commander beginning in the Civil War.*

Custer and the Seventh soon returned to a new fort just south of Bismarck. Originally called Fort McKeen, the newly constructed fort overlooked the Missouri River bottom and was named Fort Abraham Lincoln. Libbie joined Custer there and together they settled into a new house.

The next spring, General Sheridan visited Custer from his Chicago headquarters. At some point, the two decided to get approval from Washington for an exploratory trip into the Black Hills. Rumors of gold in the Black Hills had been so persistent they they thought it time to see for themselves.

In the summer, with General Sherman's approval, Sheridan ordered the Army on a march into the Black Hills, land that by treaty belonged to the Indians. The Treaty of 1868 said: "No white person or persons shall be permitted to settle upon or occupy any portion of the territory, or without the consent of the Indians to pass through the same." But the Army exercised a special provision whereby they could go in, ignoring the treaty.

This Black Hills expedition was made up of ten companies of the Seventh Cavalry, two companies of infantry, photographer W.H. Illingworth, Yale ethnologist George Bird Grinnell, two experienced gold miners and President U.S. Grant's son Frederick Dent Grant. There were over one hundred wagons and ambulances, a herd of beef cattle, three Gatling guns and a three-inch cannon. For the first time, Boston Custer, George's youngest brother, was along on the trip.

On July 20, 1874, the Seventh entered the beautiful pine-forested hills. Custer and those with him explored the natural beauty of the area for nineteen days. On August 3, Custer ordered scout Charley Reynolds to ride to Fort Laramie with official reports and news releases. By the end of August the nation's newspapers proclaimed that gold was in the Black Hills. On August 30, the Seventh marched into Fort Abraham Lincoln, the band playing the "Garry Owen." And by the summer of 1875, thousands were pouring into the Black Hills in search of Custer's Gold. The Army attempted to keep them out, but as the New York *Tribune* stated: "If there is gold in the Black Hills, no army on earth can keep the adventurous men of the west out of them."

Summer 1875 was dull at Fort Abraham Lincoln. Many thought the Seventh should have been sent to keep whites out of the Black Hills, but no one asked for them. Late in the summer, Secretary of War William Worth Belknap visited Fort Abraham Lincoln but Custer wasn't impressed. When the post trader at Fort Abraham Lincoln demanded unreasonable prices and Custer dispatched officers to Bismarck to buy the goods cheaper, Secretary Belknap ordered that Custer stop this. As a result, when Belknap visited in the fall of 1875, Custer snubbed him. After the '73 and '74 expeditions, 1875 was indeed a letdown.

Custer took a two-month leave in the fall, subsequently taking two extensions, but was refused by Secretary of War Belknap when he requested a third. He returned to Fort Abraham Lincoln in February. Then he was called to Washington, D.C., to testify before a Congressional hearing on corruption in the Grant Administration. Custer, in his book *My Life on the Plains* (the *Galaxy* articles about 1867–68), was critical of the Grant Administration's Indian policy. The Democrats, for the first time since the Civil War, had control of the House. They had initiated an investigation into charges of Republican corruption. Since it appeared Secretary of War Belknap had been selling Indian post-traderships, and since Custer knew prices at the sutler's store at Fort Abraham Lincoln were unreasonably high, and since he did not personally like Secretary Belknap, Custer was eager to testify in the so-called Indian Ring matter.

As it turned out, he had no information that could be used, but his scatter-gun approach on the witness stand included accusations about President Grant's brother Orvil, angering President Grant. It looked for a time as if Custer would not return to Dakota Territory in time to join the new attack on the Indians that had been in the planning for several months.

This new trouble began when the Sioux Indians refused to sell the Black Hills and other lands to the United States. An order was issued in the fall of 1875 which demanded that the Indians be on reservations by January 31, 1876, or they'd be deemed hostile and the Army would come shooting. It was virtually impossible for the Indians to meet the deadline, so on February 7, 1876, General Sherman ordered General Sheridan to plan military operations against the hostiles in the Black Hills region. And so, General Sheridan, who liked winter operations, sent General George Crook and a column of nine hundred north from Fort Laramie, Wyoming. As soon as they could march, Colonel John Gibbon and 450 soldiers were to come from Fort Shaw and Fort Ellis in Montana and a force of nearly a thousand would come from Fort Abraham Lincoln.

Custer had hoped to command the column from Fort Abraham Lincoln, but he was stuck in Washington, D.C. He tried to see the President and was refused. Newspapers picked up on the issue and insinuated that Grant was getting revenge. Anyhow, an irate Custer left for Dakota Territory without proper orders and when his train got to Chicago, he was arrested.

Custer wrote the President, "I appeal to you as a soldier to spare me the humiliation of seeing my regiment march to meet the enemy and I not share the dangers." In addition, Major General Alfred Howe Terry, commanding the Department of the Dakota, intervened, insisting that they needed Custer. General Sherman, the commander of the Army, and Custer's old friend General Sheridan convinced President Grant to permit it, and together Terry and Custer rode west to Fort Abraham Lincoln. But Terry was to command the column from there and no newspapermen were to accompany Custer.

General Crook's column of about nine hundred men plowed through cold, snow and ice until about March 17th. They'd struck an Indian trail and Crook sent Colonel Joseph J. Reynolds and 300 men to strike the little village. There were just over a hundred Sioux and Cheyenne lodges and Reynolds quickly overran them. In bitter cold, however, the Indians counterattacked and sent Reynolds and Crook scampering back to Wyoming. Crook decided to wait until the weather warmed some.

In April, Gibbon and six companies of the Seventh Infantry and four of the Second Cavalry marched east. On May 17, ex-lawyer General Alfred Terry and Custer marched out of Fort Abraham Lincoln for a long ride over the rain-sogged Plains to the Yellowstone River where they were to join with Gibbon. Twelve companies (they were not officially "troops" until 1883) of the Seventh Cavalry, about 700 men; two companies of the Seventeenth Infantry and one of the Sixth; a platoon of Gatling guns from the Twentieth Infantry; 150 wagons and a beef herd marched out of Fort Abraham Lincoln to the music of "The Girl I Left Behind Me."

There were civilians along too, including Custer's brother Boston Custer, who went along as forage master and Custer's nephew Henry Armstrong (Autie) Reed, who helped drive the beef herd. And for the first day and night of the march, Custer's wife Libbie and sister Margaret Calhoun rode along. And there were Crow and Arikaree Indian scouts. The Crows were in native dress; the forty Arikaree wore Army uniforms.

On May 18, after the paymaster paid Custer's soldiers, Libbie and Margaret followed him back to Fort Abraham Lincoln. After twelve years of marriage, this was the last time Libbie would see her husband. She lived until 1933, a devoted widow to Custer and his memory for nearly fifty-seven years.

Scouts from Terry's and Gibbon's columns found each other on June 3 and over the next couple weeks they continued on to a June 21 rendezvous at the mouth of Rosebud Creek on the Yellowstone River.

In the meantime, Custer scouted up the Little Missouri and found nothing. Major Marcus Reno scouted up the Powder River then crossed to the Tongue and Rosebud and back to the rendezvous point. Reno reported finding the trail of a 300-lodge village.

Unknown to the Gibbon-Terry forces at the mouth of Rosebud Creek, there was a fight on June 17th about 75 miles southwest between warriors from the Indian camp and Crook's command.

Crook had come out again when the weather warmed, but he'd changed the makeup of his force. Instead of five companies of the Third Cavalry, he now had ten to go with five from the Second Cavalry. He'd also added three companies of the Ninth Infantry to go with two from the Fourth. Crook's column now had a thousand pack mules and 120 wagons. He brought along 176 Crow and 86 Shoshoni scouts. He'd faced the enemy in March. He wanted more strength.

The fight 75 miles up Rosebud Creek on June 17 lasted several hours with the Indians finally withdrawing. Crook then wheeled his army and headed back to Wyoming and a supply camp on Goose Creek near present Sheridan. He still wasn't strong enough.

Terry and Gibbon figured the big village Reno had discovered evidence of had crossed west over the divide to the area of the river called Little Bighorn. In a meeting aboard the steamboat *Far West* on June 21, they figured they might be up against 1,000 to 1,500 warriors and the biggest problem they faced was keeping them from escaping. Their plan: Custer and the Seventh would trace the Rosebud to the Indian trail. Gibbon's men would be ferried to the south side of the Yellowstone, then march along the bank to the mouth of the Bighorn and up that river. The *Far West* would accompany them as long as the Bighorn was navigable. Together, Custer and Gibbon would trap the Indians between them.

Custer's men, in preparation for the march, bought tobacco and snuff. Some bought straw hats and checkered shirts to help ward off the heat. The sutler also had whiskey for sale.

On June 22 at noon, Custer and his men passed in review. Each man carried twelve pounds of oats in a grain bag on the cantle of his saddle. Each had a haversack filled with rations.

The Seventh's orange-bordered blue saddle blankets added color to the parade. Custer didn't take the Gatling guns, but had about 600 men along. And as Custer rode by, Gibbon called, "Now, Custer, don't be greedy, but wait for us."

"No," Custer replied, "I will not."

The Seventh marched twelve miles that first day and went into camp. Up at dawn, they marched at 5 a.m. It was not a good march, although they did make thirty-three miles that day. The heat, the flies and the alkaline dust combined to make the men miserable. Their horses kicked up clouds of the choking dust, but when they could see, the red-rock rimmed Rosebud Valley was beautiful.

And they found Indian sign everywhere. Camp circles were many and frequent. The Indian trail was a wide one where the women, children, old men and their travois poles fanned out as they moved through the country. There was hardly any grass. The Indian ponies had clipped it to the ground. It was a big herd. Mitch Bouyer, a half-breed scout, told a young officer, "Well, I can tell you we are going to have a damned big fight."

On the 24th, they turned with the Indian trail to the west. There were more camp circles and a place where there'd been a sundance celebration. Pony droppings along the Indian trail were fresher. Custer pushed harder and after 28 miles and a halt at sundown, he ordered another march, riding again at 11 p.m. They made ten miles by 2 a.m. It was now Sunday, June 25, 1876.

Weary cavalrymen slid off their horses and unsaddled the jaded animals. The heat and dust brought sores on some of the mounts. Some soldiers rubbed the horses down with grass. Others sought only the soothing solace of sleep.

Custer and his scouts spotted the Indian village at dawn. It lay some fifteen miles to their west along the Little Bighorn River. Soon

*Custer (second from left) is shown in 1874 with a grizzly he shot. To Custer's right is Bloody Knife, the Arikaree scout killed with Reno.*

the Seventh was mounted and riding toward the crest of the divide. They crossed about noon and started the downhill trip to the valley of the Little Bighorn.

It was about this time that a sergeant reported seeing Sioux Indians along the trail they'd traveled. He'd gone after a missing box of hardtack that had fallen from a pack mule. He found the hardtack and three Indians trying to break open the box. He ran them off, then reported to Custer.

For the first time in two days, Custer told buglar Giovanni Martini to sound officer's call. It was at this meeting that Custer divided his forces. Reno took a group, Frederick Benteen another and Custer another. Captain Thomas M. McDougall and B Company were assigned to stay back and protect the pack train.

There was unrest by now among some with Custer. Bloody Knife, an Arikaree and a favorite of Custer, warned, "We'll find enough Sioux to keep fighting two or three days."

Custer smiled, "Oh, I guess we'll get through them in one day."

Bloody Knife didn't believe it. Later he made his prayers and bade farewell to the sun: "I shall not see you go down behind the hills tonight."

Mitch Bouyer, another scout, could only say, "If we go in there, we will never come out."

Custer and Reno rode down Ash Creek and came to an Indian tipi on fire. An interpreter, Frank Girard, spotted about forty Indians ahead. He yelled, "Here are your Indians — running like devils."

Custer ordered the Indian scouts to give chase, but the scouts refused. Custer then ordered Reno to attack, adding that he'd support him with "the whole outfit."

Reno's detachment charged toward the river as ordered, crossing the Little Bighorn and turning toward the village. Some time later, Reno's men were repelled and forced to escape back across the river and to the top of what would later be called Reno's Hill.

While this was going on, Custer led over 200 men northeast, stopping briefly to water the horses in a branch of Ash Creek. Continuing on, Captain Thomas W. Custer (Company C), Lieutenant James Calhoun (Company L), Captain Myles W. Keough (Company I), Captain George W. Yates (Company F), and Lieutenant Algernon E. Smith (Company E) and their companies strung out behind Custer. He rode more or less parallel to the high bluffs on the northerly side of the Little Bighorn. Then he halted his men and rode to the bluff, a flat plateau-like area, overlooking the valley.

From there Custer took out his glasses and looked all around. He could see only a few hundred lodges. There were women, children and dogs moving around. The village wasn't running. That was good! He turned in his saddle and called out to his men, "Hurrah, boys, we've got them!"

What Custer didn't realize was that in the valley, hidden from his view by the terrain, was a huge village several miles long, containing perhaps 1,500 lodges and countless temporary shelters called wickiups. There were over 10,000 Indians and probably four or five thousand warriors.

The Indians not only outnumbered Custer, but some would argue that the Indians were better armed. While Custer's command used the Model 1873 .45–70 single-shot Springfield "trapdoor" carbines and .45 Colt Peacemaker revolvers, the Indians used .50 caliber models like the Sharps carbine or the 1866, 1869 and 1870 Springfields. There is evidence that they used the Henry rifle, the 1873 .44–40 Winchester carbine, and the 1866 Winchester too. Crazy Horse, the Oglala Sioux warrior, owned an 1866 Winchester carbine and Sitting Bull, the Hunkpapa Sioux medicine man often packed an 1873 Winchester carbine. Some of these were repeaters, good rifles. On the other hand, the Springfield carbines carried by Custer's men had a bad habit. Sometimes the ejector did not throw out the spent shell case. A pocket knife was needed then to dig the case out of the chamber. But it seldom misfired and had a range that discouraged bow-and-arrow or musket fire.

Custer wore two ivory-handled English .450 Webley self-cocking revolvers with rings in the butts for lanyards. He had a hunting knife in a beaded, fringed scabbard and a canvas cartridge belt. His buckskin suit was fringed on the sleeves and legs. Under the suit, he wore a double-breasted military shirt. He also carried a .50 caliber Remington Rolling-block Sporting Rifle, probably the same one he'd received from the Remington Company in 1872.

Anyhow, after viewing the village, Custer rode back to the column and ordered them to continue on, this time at a faster pace. When they came to the head of a big ravine now called Medicine Tail Coulee that led down to the river, Custer decided to send a message.

Earlier he'd dispatched Sergeant Daniel Kanipe to hurry along the pack train. Now, he called to his bugler, Giovanni Martini, "Orderly, I want you to take a message to Colonel Benteen. Ride as fast as you can and tell him to hurry. Tell him it's a big village and I want him to be quick, and to bring the ammunition packs."

Martini nodded and started to ride away. Lieutenant William W. Cooke, Custer's adjutant, called, "Wait, orderly, I'll give you a message."

Cooke wrote the message on a page in a small notebook, tore it out, handed it to Martini and watched as the bugler kicked his horse into action and back along the trail the Custer column had just traveled.

Martini rode flat out, but looked back to see Custer's column galloping into the ravine. When he was farther away, he heard shooting and looked again. This time, he saw Indians, "Some waving buffalo robes and some shooting. They had been in ambush," he remembered later.

That was the last Martini saw of Custer. The speeding messenger laid low in the saddle and shot over the grassy hills, Indian bullets whizzing after him and one slamming into his horse's rump.

On the way, Martini met a rider, Custer's younger brother Boston, racing toward his brother's position so as not to miss the action. Boston'd come up from the pack train. Minutes later, Martini delivered his message to Captain Benteen. It is doubtful that Custer got much farther down Medicine Tail Coulee. The apparent massive force of Sioux and Cheyenne warriors more than likely turned Custer's badly outnumbered column north uphill along a ridge where he may have deployed his brother-in-law, Margaret's husband Lieutenant James Calhoun and L Company, all riding bay horses. Then a little farther along that ridge, Captain Myles Keough and I Company, riding bays, made a stand and Captain George Yates' First Platoon set up nearby. Yates' F Company was also riding bay-colored horses. Just to the south of Custer's hill, Yates' Second Platoon and Captain Tom Custer and C Company, riding sorrels, and Lieutenant Algernon Smith's grey horse troop, E Company, tried to defend.

And then there was great confusion. Dust churned up by hundreds of ponies choked Sioux and Cheyenne warriors and soldiers alike. Dead and dying horses, soldiers and warriors lay strewn about, gunsmoke so thick those still alive weren't sure at what they were shooting.

Somewhere at sometime in all the turmoil, stunned soldiers, shocked and frightened, suddenly knew they'd die here. Some no doubt fumbled with weapons, hurrying an old shell case out, trying to get a fresh cartridge in. When a puff of wind briefly cleared the smoke and dust, a soldier saw friends laying dead, eyes staring, blood oozing from bullet holes. And there were those who were shot, once, twice, three times and to their surprise, still lived, firing sometimes at ghosts it seemed. Always there were the eerie inhuman screams from the attacking warriors adding to the horror of it all. Or were they the bloody screams of wounded soldiers, terror stricken, trying to ward off death?

At some point in all this, George Armstrong Custer felt a thud in his left chest. It probably knocked him down and blood quickly flowed from the large hole. Most agree the bullet was just under the heart, so he probably lived for a time, emptying his pistols at the terrible confusion around him. And as the life oozed from him, he slumped, sat and died. Later, a bullet struck him in the left temple.

Downhill toward the Little Bighorn, perhaps two hundred yards away, lay Boston Custer and young Autie Reed. Tom Custer was with his men, dead.

The Custer star had fallen, but with it went the way of life of a people, the Plains Indians of the American West. Their tipis would never be so rich; the buffalo would never be as many; their lives would never be so full and happy. Their ways died like Custer.

In losing, Custer had won. The citizens of the United States supported the government's efforts to force the Indians onto the reservations and to sell the lands that had been promised them less than a decade earlier.

To the day she died in 1933, Elizabeth Custer defended the actions of her husband that Sunday in Montana. He was her hero, her champion. In dying there on that dusty ridge overlooking the largest Plains Indians camp ever assembled, Custer had stamped his name indelibly into the history of his nation, a fate for which he no doubt would have traded his life.

# 3    Marcus A. Reno: Reno's Luck

Lieutenant Colonel George Armstrong Custer halted his command, stood in his stirrups, squinted up at the blistering sun directly overhead, then to one of his staff made the most disastrous decision of his 36 years. Custer ordered that his Seventh U.S. Cavalry be broken into three battalions.

The date was Sunday, June 25, 1876. Within a few hours, the Seventh Cavalry would collide with perhaps 4,000 Sioux and Cheyenne warriors. When the dust, smoke and thunder of guns ceased, Custer and his battalion of 215 would be dead; 47 more from Major Marcus A. Reno's unit would also die there on the Little Bighorn River. That then was Custer's Last Stand, one of the most devastating defeats ever suffered by American military men.

In splitting his command, Custer kept five companies for himself and sent Captain Frederick W. Benteen and 125 men (three companies: H, D, and K) to sweep south of the river valley. To Major Marcus A. Reno, he assigned about 140 men in companies A, G, and M and ordered them to continue parallel to Custer's westerly march.

Not long after, with the forest of tipis a few miles ahead, Custer ordered Major Reno to cross the river and attack the southeast end of what was probably the largest village of native people to assemble in the American West.

From a distance of two miles, Reno's command trotted, then galloped toward its destiny. It was Reno's first action against the Sioux or any other western tribe. But his record for leadership and bravery had been set long ago in more civilized savagery, the Civil War.

April 1861 found Marcus Reno one of fifteen men from Illinois who had graduated from the United States Military Academy at West Point. By the fall of 1861 he was captain of the First Cavalry. Reno rode in McClellan's Peninsular Campaign in 1862 and had his horse shot from under him in March 1863 near Kellysville, Virginia. For the gallant and meritorious services at Kelly's Ford, he was breveted Major.

The next year in October, during action at Cedar Creek in Virginia, Reno was cited for gallant and meritorious service. His record was exemplary throughout the war and when he was mustered out in July 1865, he was a brevet Colonel in the Regular Army and brevet Brigadier General of U.S. Volunteers.

From 1865 to 1875, Reno saw no action, serving mainly on staff and detached duty. He was Assistant Instructor of Infantry Tactics at West Point and later head of the New Orleans Freedman's Bureau. He was promoted to Major during December 1868. During 1870, Reno was on a long scout through Kansas and Colorado. His summers of 1873 and 1874 were spent as escort commander for the Northern Boundary Survey. And when he arrived at Fort Abraham Lincoln in Dakota Territory to join Custer in October 1875, "his record . . . was solid and his character unblemished."

Now in 1876, this expedition against the Sioux and Cheyenne and "other hostile tribes" began during May. The tribes were ordered to the reservations during the winter, but could not obey because of the extreme cold and snow. The Army went after them during March and April, but the weather turned the soldiers back. Finally on May 17, Custer's Cavalry marched west out of Fort Abraham Lincoln. They were a force of 925 officers and men.

By June 21, they bivouacked at the mouth of Rosebud Creek in Montana not far from their destination, the Little Bighorn. Meetings were held with General Alfred Terry and Colonel John Gibbon, who had arrived from Fort Ellis to the west. General Terry and Gibbon's column planned to move up the Yellowstone River, the Bighorn and Little Bighorn while Custer followed the Rosebud in search of the Sioux and Cheyenne. General George Crook, according to Terry, would join them from the south and Fort Fetterman in Wyoming. Together the three columns would crush the hostile tribes.

The next day, June 22, Custer's column passed in review for Terry, then headed south along the Rosebud. The rose-colored cliffs glowed

*Marcus A. Reno.*

in the noonday sun as 31 officers, 585 enlisted men, 40 Indian scouts, and 20 packers, guides and civilians prodded their horses down the grassy valley. Best estimates at the meeting the night before put the hostile force at less than a thousand warriors. Each soldier carried 100 rounds of carbine ammunition and 24 rounds for his pistol. The pack mules carried another 50 carbine rounds per man.

They made twelve miles that first day and 33 the 23rd. On Saturday, the 24th, they rode 28 miles during the day, then another ten miles that night. This brought Custer's Dakota Column within fifteen miles of their fate.

The column struck the enemy trail on the 23rd. The scouts warned that it was a big camp that Custer followed. The same warning was issued the morning of June 25. Custer's favorite Arikaree scout, Bloody Knife, feared the worst. Charley Reynolds, Custer's chief scout, had premonitions of death. And there were others. The signs were bad. But Custer seemed to ignore the warnings.

After leaving Reno, Custer and companies C, E, F, I, and L (215 men) made their way along the northerly bank of the Little Bighorn, leaving Reno (with 140 men) to his own devices.

Now Reno, his command still on a gallop and aiming at the south end of the hostile village, suddenly noted great swarms of mounted warriors coming directly at him, their naked, bronzed bodies shining in the afternoon sun. He was outnumbered! His command was in trouble!

Instinctively, Reno ordered his command to halt, then signaled for them to fight on foot. Every fourth man held four horses, the others kneeling at nine-foot intervals, their carbines ready. They commenced firing when the attackers were too far away. But that was not a problem for long. The screaming horde was on them, dashing recklessly close, arrows and bullets clouding the air. For about 15 minutes, according to some estimates, this devastating assault continued.

Reno, in an interview later, said, "I was convinced I had at least ten to one against me." When asked how many Sioux Reno faced that day, a seasoned sergeant replied, "You take a stick and stir up a big ant hill; stir it up good and get the ants excited and mad. Then try to count them."

Conditions worsened, the Sioux and Cheyenne riders flanking Reno's men, forcing them to desperate measures. Reno ordered a right flanking movement into a line of trees and bushes along the river. Reno remembered later, "The stream was fringed, as usual, with the trees of the plains—a growth of large cottonwoods, and on the opposite side was a range of high bluffs which had been cut into very deep ravines by the surface water and by the action of the stream. Just at their base the earth had fallen in and left perpendicular banks, making what is known as cutbanks."

Everywhere there was confusion. The warriors took advantage of the scattered forces, weaving in and out of the brush.

Bloody Knife, Custer's Arikaree scout, accompanied Reno and now Reno sought his advice. What did the Sioux plan to do next? Lives depended on Reno's next command. His own life depended on his next command!

And then it happened.

Reno was using sign language, his and Bloody Knife's arms and hands flitting over the symbols that might save their lives. All of a sudden, Bloody Knife's head exploded! The sound was a dull thud. The bronze head blew apart and slivers of bone and flecks of brain and blood sprayed Reno's face. His hands leaped to his face to wipe away the blood and the. . . . Fear and panic struck him, his body shuddering. And perhaps in that instant, his past flashed before his eyes.

In the instant that Reno's hand rushed to his face and brought away the blood and bone that had once been Bloody Knife, Reno's mind was made up. He screamed commands. Some say he rapidly ordered them to mount, dismount and mount again. The Sioux and Cheyenne darted in and out, deadly close. Reno was done with this position. Hatless, he mounted and kicked his horse southeast along the Little Bighorn, still shouting at his men to follow.

The dash for safety, a charge, Reno called it, was devastating. The Sioux mingled with the fleeing soldiers; there was no covering fire. Confusion and death rode with Reno's command.

When Reno had ridden about a mile, he reined his mount into the Little Bighorn and lunged across toward the 300-foot ridge on the northeast side of the river that led to safety. Fording the river, the riders and horses climbed a steep five-foot cutbank. All the time, the enemy whittled away at Reno's tired, scared soldiers.

Although Reno's wounded were abandoned and his retreat militarily unsound, Reno nevertheless was in the midst of an heroic effort; it was a last grasp at survival. Within minutes he and his men struggled frantically up the 300-foot incline. Of the 130 or so that went into battle with Reno less than 100 still lived. And in their frustration, Reno and his weary men wondered aloud: Where was Custer?

Shots cracked from about four miles away. (Later a Sioux warrior described the shooting by slapping his hands rapidly together.) That would be Custer, they guessed. The shooting from afar continued. A short time later Captain Benteen joined Reno, as did the pack train.

Benteen had ridden about fifteen miles, found no Indians and swung his column back to where he picked up the Seventh's trail along Ash Creek. There, he'd met Captain Thomas M. McDougall who with B Company was guarding the pack train. Benteen then rode on toward the Little Bighorn. About two miles past the burning tipi Sergeant Daniel Kanipe of Company C, Tom Custer's company, rode up to him, his horse at a gallop, and called out, "We've got 'em, boys." Custer had sent him with orders to send the mules loaded with ammunition. Benteen had sent Kanipe on to inform the pack train. He was met a mile later by another messenger from Custer. The message scrawled on paper read: "Benteen—Come on. Big village. Be quick. Bring packs. W.W. Cooke P.S. Bring pacs." Cooke, Custer's adjutant, had written it.

A short time later, Benteen came up on Reno who was just arriving at Reno's Hill, the Indians in hot pursuit. Some insisted they ride to help Custer, but Reno rejected the idea. Finally Captain Thomas Weir led a company of men along the ridge toward the shooting. They soon learned the folly of their march. The Sioux and Cheyenne swarmed after them. Weir wisely retreated the mile back to Reno's Hill.

Only then did the soldiers realize the enormity of what they faced. Perhaps 1,500 tipis stood in the valley; the pony herd on the hills the other side of the camp was the largest anyone had ever seen. Someone noticed too that the far-away shooting had ceased.

With the men from the pack train and Benteen's battalion, Reno's command now numbered 350 atop the hill. Charley Reynolds, Custer's chief scout, lay dead in the bottom near the river, a pile of empty cartridges beside his mutilated body. And there were others, nearly a half-hundred. The sniping at the soldiers on the hill continued until dark. Then a strange quiet settled over the position held by Reno's men only to be interrupted not long after by drums and chanting from the enemy camp nearly three miles downstream. Great fires glowed in the night sky.

On Reno's Hill, the men dug rifle pits with cups, knives and forks in preparation for what daylight would surely bring. They piled discarded packs and dead horses around their pits— and they prayed.

The shooting woke some early on June 26. There were a few sprinkles from the overcast, but that soon ended and the clouds sped away letting in the blazing sun. Thirst and fear made the morning hours miserable. The wounded set up a howl for water and dead horses ripened as the day wore on. Shortly after noon the attack slowed and, by evening, strangely ceased. About 7 p.m., the Sioux-Cheyenne camp fired the prairie, great clouds of smoke billowing, blocking a good view of their retreat southwest toward the Big Horn Mountains. The siege was ended.

The next morning General Terry's column rode down from the north. On Custer's hill overlooking the site where the huge Sioux-Cheyenne village stood, there lay 216 dead. Reno's losses were 47 killed, 53 wounded.

Almost immediately, there were those who began looking for a scapegoat. Major Reno, next in command, seemed the logical choice. Reno's official report in the *Annual Report of the Secretary of War for 1876,* Vol. I, pp. 477–479, lays the cause of the defeat as: 1) the division of the regiment, 2) the rapid march during two days prior to the fight, and 3) the overabundance of Indians. One author quickly accused Reno and Reno answered the charge by calling for a court of inquiry. The court convened in Chicago during January 1879 and lasted for 26 days. After 1,300 pages of testimony from twenty-three witnesses (all underwent cross-examination), the court exonerated Reno of any blame. Those who opposed Reno branded the outcome an Army whitewash.

Fellow West Pointer James Barnett Fry, who also hailed from Reno's Carrollton, Illinois hometown, was severely critical of Reno and made several bitter attacks. In a January 1892 *Century Magazine* article, Fry accused Reno of not conducting himself properly. Fry thought Reno should have ridden to the sound of gunfire.

Other critics, usually Custer promoters, were out to protect Custer's obvious foolhardiness in guiding his command to its destruction.

On the other hand, Reno did little to help his cause. Within just a few days of the Custer Fight, he became embroiled in a "public exchange." According to some he began to behave with extraordinary rashness and unpleasantness. There were those who blamed some of these troubles on his drinking. Others blamed Reno's conduct on his wife's untimely death during July 1874. (Mary Hanna Ross, daughter of a prominent Harrisburg, Pennsylvania businessman, married Reno during the Civil War. She died while Reno was on escort duty. When Reno asked to be relieved so he could return to the East, the Army denied his request. To them was born a son, Robert Ross Reno.)

Regardless, on July 24, 1876, Reno was placed under arrest. The charges remain unknown, since there is no existing record. Reports during August show difficulties with his staff. And there was an incident at the Officer's Club Room at Fort Abraham Lincoln in September. By mid-October he was relieved of command. And during December he was made commander of a rundown fort in Dakota Territory called Fort Abercrombie. It was on the west bank of the Red River of the North, thirty miles south of the present towns of Fargo, North Dakota and Moorhead, Minnesota.

From then until 1880, Reno's problems seemed to compound. Incidents with the wife of Captain James M. Bell at Fort Abercrombie led to a court-martial. It was recommended that Reno be dismissed from service, but President Rutherford Hayes, after studying Reno's record, reduced the sentence to a two-year suspension from duty without pay.

Back on duty in 1879 at Fort Meade, Dakota Territory, Reno was drinking to excess and too frequently. There were unpleasant occurrences, but none so dastardly, in the eyes of Post Commander Colonel Samuel Davis Sturgis, than Reno peeping at Sturgis' twenty-year-old daughter Ella through a window while she was "in complete toilet."

Reno apologized, but Sturgis had had enough and on April 1, 1880, Reno was dishonorably discharged from service for "Conduct to the Prejudice of Good Order and Military Discipline." (This, despite the fact that five of the seven court-martial judges recommended clemency.)

On March 29, 1889, a few days short of the ninth anniversary of his removal from the Army, Marcus A. Reno died at Providence Hospital in Washington, D.C., following an operation for cancer of the tongue. To his death, he was a bitter man.

On May 31, 1967, the Office of Assistant Secretary of Defense (Public Affairs), the Pentagon, issued the following statement:

"The Secretary of the Army has directed that all Department of the Army records of Marcus A. Reno be corrected to show that he was honorably discharged from the United States Army in the grade of Major, United States Army (Brevet Colonel, United States Army, and Brevet Brigadier General, United States Volunteers) on 1 April 1880. The Secretary's action was in response to an application submitted by Mr. Charles Reno, the great grandnephew of Major Reno."

Not long after, Major Reno's body was removed from a sunken, unmarked grave in Washington, D.C. and removed to its rightful place of honor in the national cemetery at the Custer Battlefield National Monument.

# 4           Reno's Early Life

Marcus Reno's family arrived in Greene County, Illinois about forty miles north of St. Louis, Missouri from Tennessee. The name Reno was originally Reynaud, from the French. James Reno, Marcus' father, was the son of Aaron (1780–1860) and Nancy Reno. Not long after arrival, James married a divorcee from Apple Creek Prairie, just north of Carrollton, Illinois. Her name was Charlotte Hinton Miller. Besides Marcus, James and Charlotte's children were: Eliza, Leonard Warren, Cornelia, Sophronia and Henry Clinton.

In 1831 James Reno operated an inn in Carrollton and in 1833, when the town was incorporated, he was one of the first trustees, as was Edward Dickinson Baker, later a close friend of Abraham Lincoln (Lincoln's son, Edward, was named for Baker).

Marcus' father owned and operated a hotel for a while, was elected clerk of Greene County, and served as postmaster. The Panic of 1837 hurt him financially, but by 1844 he was recovering. He formed a partnership and opened a dry goods store (Reno & Simpson) during 1847. And two months after Marcus' mother died in June 1848, James Reno moved ten miles north to White Hall and opened, with his brother, the largest dry goods and drug store in the area.

In January 1849, James Reno died. He was 47 years old. Burial was in Carrollton's city cemetery beside his wife. Marcus Reno was only 14 at the time. He and his younger brothers and sisters lived with his brother-in-law and sister, Robert and Cornelia Hance. Young Marcus worked for his father's former partner, Dr. French Simpson, and during 1851 came under the guardianship of his mother's brother, Alfred Hinton. It was during that year that he received his appointment (probably from Congressman Edward Dickinson Baker) to the United States Military Academy.

It took Reno six years and he amassed a record 1,031 demerits, but in 1857 he became little Carrollton's third resident to graduate West Point.

He was assigned to the Pacific Northwest until the Civil War began.

# 5     Charles A. Reynolds: The Death of Lonesome Charley

Crow's Nest, Montana Territory, June 25, 1876—Chief of Scouts Charley Reynolds lay quietly studying the land between him and the horizon, the mountains. At dawn from this high lookout butte with slopes of gray rock, dappled with jack pines and scattered cedar, he could look for miles in all directions, searching for sign of the Indian camp. It was a great day, a day to fire the brave and gain new glories. And for Charley Reynolds, it was a good day to die.

Reynolds scouted for Lieutenant Colonel George Armstrong Custer and was one of nearly a thousand fighting men that marched out of Fort Abraham Lincoln, Dakota Territory to the tunes of Custer's favorite, "Garry Owen," and everyone's favorite, "The Girl I Left Behind Me," on May 17, 1876, to locate and punish Indians, Sioux and Cheyenne in particular, considered hostile. Commanded by General Alfred H. Terry, the column trailed west from Dakota into Montana Territory to the Yellowstone River, Reynolds guiding the column. At the mouth of the Rosebud a base camp was established and Custer was ordered south with about 600 men. They rode up the creek and then west, following the Indian trail discovered June 23. In a diary entry, Charley Reynolds wrote, "passed several (abandoned) Indian camps the first of which was about 20 days old the Indians seemed to be traveling leisurely (sic) along, last camp was probably 12 days old." Reynolds did not record that the trail was a half-mile wide! (Actually, Reynolds seems to be a day behind in this diary that has its last entry on June 22. Custer's column struck the Indian trail on the 23rd. This diary is in the possession of the Minnesota Historical Society.)

Just thirty-four years old, Reynolds was born in Warren County, Illinois, on March 20, 1842, to physician Joseph Boyer Reynolds and the former Phebe Bush. He attended grammar school and Abingdon College before moving to Pardee, Kansas in 1859.

With the Tenth Kansas Regiment during the Civil War he traveled the Santa Fe Trail. (Actually, Reynolds joined Company B, 4th Regiment, Kansas Volunteers, but they subsequently became the Tenth.) Following the war, a trading venture collapsed when Indians killed his partner. He became a hunter, making a profession of it. He was good enough that some Indians dubbed him "Hunter-Who-Never-Goes-Out-For-Nothing." Others called him "Lucky Man." Because he often preferred hunting alone, many knew him simply as "Lonesome Charley." And so, the five foot, eight inch, shy, soft-spoken Charley Reynolds seemed always to perform the impossible, creating in his lifetime stories that nearly made him a legend.

Reynolds was in demand as a guide and scout for expeditions into Montana Territory during the 1870s. It was on an 1873 expedition that he met Lieutenant Colonel George Armstrong Custer. The following year, Custer selected him as chief scout for the Black Hills Expedition. In 1875, Reynolds guided Corps of Engineers Colonel William Ludlow's reconnaissance of Yellowstone Park and Judith Basin. It was on this 1875 trip that Reynolds befriended Colonel Philetus W. Norris.

Norris and Reynolds met in August 1875 at the forks of the Yellowstone River. Gathered around a cool fire that night, the two talked for hours, becoming fast friends.

The next morning Reynolds and Norris were off in separate directions, but they met again a few weeks later at a clump of cabins called Carroll, Montana. After a steamboat ride down the Missouri, the two visited old Fort Union and Fort Buford near the mouth of the Yellowstone.

Norris wrote later, "Amid the shadows of the setting sun, echoes of the evening gun at Fort Buford roused us from hours of pensive wanderings among the ruins of old Fort Union and the cemetery near Fort Buford. With a last lingering look at the turfy tomb of slaughtered friends, and with a heart too full for utterance, I was leaving the enclosure in silence when Charley, in quiet but frank and earnest manner, said, 'Comrade, I am dreaming of where a year hence will find us.' " Not long after, Norris returned home to Michigan.

In the spring of 1876, Colonel Norris invited Reynolds to the exposition in Philadelphia celebrating America's Centennial. Instead, Reynolds signed on with the Seventh U.S. Cavalry for $100 a month. This summer, Reynolds told a friend, would see "the greatest Indian battle ever fought on this continent." He planned to be there.

Now it was June 25, a Sunday. The morning sun flared color into the big sky but still was not visible above the eastern horizon. Crow and Arikaree Indian scouts now claimed they could see the Sioux camp. The Arikaree Red Star, pointing, said smoke and horses were there in the valley.

Reynolds now could see the river, the Little Bighorn, perhaps fifteen miles away. Off to the south, he scanned right, tracing the twisting, turning stream northward through the wrinkled land. At places, the green valley spread to maybe two miles, then choked down into narrow cuts between the low benches on the west and high bluffs along the east. Thickets of brush and trees defined bend after bend as the river hooked and curved its way northward to the Bighorn, then the Yellowstone River. It seemed that the Little Bighorn couldn't decide which way to flow.

No smoke; no horses. Reynolds pulled field glasses from a leather case, fitted them to his eyes, and rescanned the river's snake-like path. Then, lowering the glasses, he nodded. The wisps of smoke, the crawling black-speckled hillside—an enormous horse herd, maybe 20,000 ponies; it was a big camp.

Reynolds wrote a note to Custer, dispatched it with two Arikaree scouts, and watched breathlessly from the lookout as the scouts were almost discovered by a half dozen Sioux riders passing near their trail. Safely past the Sioux, the messengers continued on, riding toward the flat, blue-smoke cloud that marked Custer's camp.

Just after 10 a.m., Custer arrived at Crow's Nest. Reynolds, Custer, and the Indian scouts gathered at the lookout. A mounding foggy haze now lay over the valley. Custer could not see the village. He suggested that Reynolds perhaps had mistaken white buttes for tipis.

*Lonesome Charley Reynolds. (Courtesy of the Smithsonian Institution.)*

Reynolds removed his glasses and Custer took them. Seconds later, Custer nodded agreement. The village was there.

A Crow scout asked what Custer thought of the camp and a translator put the question to Custer.

"This camp," Custer replied, "has not seen our army, none of their scouts have seen us."

The Crow responded skeptically, "You say we have not been seen. These Sioux we have seen at the foot of the hill, two going one way, and four the other are good scouts, they have seen the smoke of our camp."

Custer answered sharply, "I say again we have not been seen. That camp has not seen us, I am going to carry out what I think."

Custer hesitated, removed his big gray hat and wiped away the sweat, then added, calmer now, "I want to wait until it is dark and then we will march, we will place our army around the Sioux camp."

The Crow shook his head, "That plan is bad, it should not be carried out."

Tired of the argument, Custer replied, matter-of-factly, "I have said what I propose to do, I want to wait until it is dark and then go ahead with my plan." Reynolds and the others from Crow's Nest soon joined the column and rode toward the Wolf Mountains' divide. The blazing sun stood almost overhead now and too hot. It was a slow, weary march, but a noisy one. Men were too tired to talk. They'd ridden over thirty miles on Friday, nearly thirty more Saturday, and then ten during the night. It was Sunday now. The creak of leather, the rattle of equipment, and horses snorting dust and mules braying, trumpeting their presence, set up quite a commotion.

Across the divide at the forks of Ash Creek (now Reno Creek) about noon, Custer divided the column. Captain Thomas M. McDougall took one company to guard the 150-mule pack train. Captain Frederick Benteen and three companies rode southwest across the rugged breaks of the Wolf Mountains. Custer led about 215 men northwest down Ash Creek. Parallel, across the creek, Major Marcus Reno commanded companies under Captain Thomas H. French., First Lieutenant Donald McIntosh, and Captain Myles Moylan. Since Major Reno was in the advance, Charley Reynolds and the scouts rode with him, about 150 men in all.

Two hours and ten miles later, the scouts found a lone tipi on a flat along Ash Creek. It was a burial tipi. They searched it and found the body of a dead warrior on a low scaffold. The Indian scouts set it ablaze. A band of Sioux just out of carbine range appeared and casually rode away toward the valley of the Little Bighorn.

Custer's adjutant William W. Cooke ordered Reno to go after them. The village lay just ahead and was running away, he said. "Custer says to move at as rapid a gait as you think prudent, and to charge afterward, and you will be supported by the whole outfit."

Reno ordered the charge and Second Lieutenant Charles A. Varnum, in charge of the Arikaree and Crow scouts, waved his hat and yelled, "Thirty days' furlough to the man who gets the first scalp."

That was it. There was no turning back. Charley Reynolds, like all the rest, pointed his horse downhill, locked his knees tightly, grabbed a handful of mane, and charged toward the river.

Too quickly, they were at the river. The soldiers rode into the swift water, not too deep here, but the horses were sinking in the sand bottom, slowing them as they plunged and splashed toward the bank some thirty feet away.

On the opposite bank, troopers slid from their saddles and let the weary horses drink. Soon all were dismounted, their horses sucking the cold, mountain-stream water, their bellies bulging. Most released the saddle girths. The air was hot and still.

It took about fifteen minutes to get the three companies across, the horses watered, and the saddle girths retightened for the fight that lay ahead. In addition, there was trouble with the Arikaree scouts. They reined their ponies to a halt at the river and refused to cross. Fred Girard, the Arikaree interpreter, scolded and tongue-lashed them into crossing in preparation for the coming battle. The Arikaree protested that they were hired to scout, not fight. There were stragglers among the soldiers too, but no time to wait for them. In most cases, their mounts were simply used up.

Charley Reynolds may have been having second thoughts. The great size of the trail they'd followed here was a sure warning. And the Indian scouts were all talking and signing that this was a big, the biggest camp. Before he'd ridden with Custer south from the Yellowstone River, Reynolds had visited the paddlewheeler *Far West*, captained by his friend Grant Marsh. Reynolds' hand was infected and Marsh asked him about it. Reynolds answered, "No better. Doctor Henry Porter can't seem to cure it and my hand is no use."

Marsh, concerned, told him, "See here, Charlie, I wish you would give up going with General Custer and stay on the boat. It will be a hard march for you in your condition, and you can't do any fighting anyway, with that hand."

Reynolds smiled and replied, "Captain, I've been waiting and getting ready for this expedition for two years and I would sooner be dead than miss it."

(One account has the Arikaree scout Bloody Knife telling Reynolds and others the previous night, "Myself, I know what is to happen to me; my sacred helper has given me warning that I am not to see the set of tomorrow's sun."

Reynolds nodded, agreeing quietly, "I feel as he does: tomorrow will be the end for me, too." He added, "Anyone who wants my little outfit of stuff can have it right now."

Reynolds then opened his "war sack" and began giving away tobacco, some shirts, a sewing kit.)

It was all wrong! Up the dry-bottomed valley as Reno commenced forming his companies, pale, yellow dust billowed. The village was preparing for a fight. The Indians were ready and determined to protect their women, children, and old people from these blue-coated invaders.

Reynolds looked back. Still no Custer. Custer's command must be hidden behind the bluffs standing east of them.

Reno and his officers formed a column of fours and rode for about a mile, always skirting the timber-bordered bends of the river to their right, before spreading into a jagged battle line. French's company was on the right, McIntosh on the left, and Moylan in the rear. Charley Reynolds and the other scouts were off to the left, the Indian scouts farther to his left near where the valley rose to higher ground. On order, they kicked their mounts into a trot, then a slow gallop, and charged northwest, down the Little Bighorn Valley. For most of the young troopers, the charge was too fast and they bounced recklessly in their saddles.

To their front, there was uncertainty. Bullberry bushes and trees screened the river now. Indians darted in and out of the timber by the river, setting fires at intervals, the thick, white smoke just beginning to curl up out of the cottonwood and box elder trees. Just coming into view were the bleached skins of tipis as thick as a forest, but the rolling dust made them disappear. It was apparent warriors from the big village rode toward them. Charging! No, swarming! Others amid whoops and cries ran along on foot. Riders spun their war ponies and retreated toward the village, trying to suck the raw recruits into their deadly trap. It was a terrifying sight. There were so many of the enemy.

Reno's cavalry charge slowed gradually. There was a shot nearby, probably one of the Indian scouts. Still the battle line slowed, becoming wavy. To Reynolds' right now, one soldier kept right on charging, eyes terror-filled, his entire weight in his stirrups trying to halt his runaway horse. He and the horse were swallowed up by the dusty swarm of Sioux and Cheyenne attackers.

An order to halt brought them to a standstill. Reynolds, Fred Girard, scout George Herendeen, Doctor Henry R. Porter, and the Arikaree Bloody Knife were all together. Reynolds asked Girard, "Do you have any whiskey? I never felt so in all the days of my life. I'm depressed, discouraged. I need a little stimulant."

Girard had whiskey and Reynolds took a long pull of it. Someone said he shouldn't drink too much, "We've got plenty business on our hands this day."

Then came an order to dismount and form skirmishers. Every fourth man, like clockwork, led four horses into the timber along the river, leaving perhaps eighty soldiers on line, many of them inexperienced. It was not good. Reno's first dealings with Indians were not going well. His cavalry, basically an offensive unit, now fought defensively.

Everywhere there was dust and charging warriors from the big village. There was little time now except to fire and load, fire and load. The line was under a hail of blistering bullets and hissing arrows. Some of the troopers bravely knelt and fired. Others fired from behind a breastwork of prairie dog mounds. Non-commissioned officers shouted orders that few heard.

Screaming their own words of encouragement, the mounted Sioux and Cheyenne attackers dashed in and out, their ponies brightly decorated, feathers tied and flying from their bridles and manes, their tails tied for war. Those on foot knelt and fired, then ran forward, knelt and fired again. And to everyone's surprise, the first wave from the huge Indian camp was repulsed.

Abandoning their straight-on attack, the determined warriors quickly concentrated on the left end of Reno's line. This line would not hold long. And already the left end, the end the Indian scouts and Reynolds were on, was being shoved toward the river by a large group of flanking, stubborn warriors. And now too, there was enemy behind the line. The blue smoke of gunpowder mingled with the pale yellow dust as war cries and popping guns smoothered the little band of desperate men. Things were bad and growing worse!

Someone must have given the order to withdraw to the horses in the timber because that's what Reynolds and the others suddenly realized was happening. They blazed away, their guns hot, as they retreated, wanting now badly to get to the relative safety of the trees. Still it seemed that they'd not last long there either. Already Sioux warriors slipped into the trees. Others instinctively took higher ground in the direction from where Reno's command had ridden.

Confusion, bewilderment, and a great urge to survive was present in the timber. Reno, waving a smoking pistol, his hat gone, a red bandana tied around his head, tried hard to command a thin, scattered firing line in the tangled brush. And then there was an order to mount and ride out of this place of fire, singing bullets, and chaos. A scout nearby cursed, "What damn fool move is this?"

But before Reynolds could get to a horse, a great volley of shots rattled through the woods, thwacking and whining as they skipped and slammed into trees and branches, shaking the thorny rose and plum bushes. Some of the troopers and scouts hesitated, their horses dancing crazily, scared, some wounded. A terrified horse reared and screamed through bitted teeth, blood spurting from a bullet hole in the neck. All was a shambles. Men cried; others were too scared. Fire set by the Indians crackled in the midst of popping guns. Death was everywhere.

Charley Reynolds' life, all thirty-four years of it, came down to this clump of timber, this valley of death, and these yelling, deadly Indians, their bone whistles shrilly screeching signals. Calmly though, he stood his ground and fired his weapons. (Second Lieutenant Luther B. Hare remembered seeing Reynolds. He wrote later, "I saw him several times during the fight in the bottom and, of course, noticed and was impressed by his wonderful coolness and apparent indifference to the warm fire that was being poured in on us.") Not far away Doctor Henry Porter, the surgeon, worked furiously over a wounded soldier in a cluster of bushes. The bushes around the linen-duster clad doctor shook and zipping bullets raised puffs of dust around him. Still the doctor tended the bloody soldier, not noticing.

That was not right! Reynolds jumped to his feet and screamed above the din, "Doctor, the Indians are shooting at you!"

Doctor Porter, startled, looked around. Just as he spotted Reynolds, the scout threw his hands in the air and a puff of dust spurted from his chest.

Lonesome Charley Reynolds died before he hit the ground.

In the two days that Reynolds' body lay there, the combined Sioux-Cheyenne camp of thousands successfully defended its families. Everyone in the companies with Custer — 216 soldiers and civilians — were killed. Reno lost, besides Charley Reynolds, forty-six more. He had fifty-three wounded. Benteen's unit joined Reno and together, they held out until the remainder of the command under General Alfred Terry arrived.

They found Reynolds' body on June 27. It was stripped; the head was gone. Some say there were sixty spent cartridges where he lay. (Lieutenant Hare recalled, "I saw him after his death and my recollection is that he was buried by the detail that I was in charge of, or it may have been done by the detail that (Lt. George D.) Wallace had charge of, for we were working together. At any rate he was killed in the bottom and buried there."

Various monuments marked Reynolds' death site (This was said in the 1920s to be "about one mile southeast of the present railroad station of Garryowen, along the Burlington Railroad.") until a granite stone was placed by a local Lion's Club in 1938. The body ("A few small bones; fragments of his hat and clothing; and a few tufts of his known auburn hair") was gathered into a handkerchief in 1877 and removed by Colonel Philetus W. Norris, the second superintendent of Yellowstone Park, and probably buried in Norris' family plot near Ann Arbor, Michigan.

Norris wrote, "The gallant Charley Reynolds (was) moral, temperate, mild and quiet, until emergency called forth the matchless nerve and daring that made him the leading shot and scout of the Missouri and Yellowstone."

"As a hunter and scout," wrote William F. "Buffalo Bill" Cody, "he ranked with the best."

Custer's wife, Elizabeth, wrote of Reynolds, "Had he worn all the insignia of the high rank and the decorations of an adoring country, he could not have led a braver life or died a more heroic death."

# 6     Sitting Bull: Hunkpapa Sioux

Sunday, June 25, 1876—The Indian Camp, Little Bighorn River, Montana Territory.

Sitting Bull slept late the morning of June 25, 1876. The great camp, a forest of tipis, stretched six miles, curving in and out, hugging the many twists and turns of the Little Bighorn, the stream the Sioux called the Greasy Grass. Farthest down river, to the northwest, stood the Cheyenne lodges. Then came the Oglalas, Sans Arcs, Blackfeet Sioux and Minneconjous. The Hunkpapas, Sitting Bull's people, were at the other, the southernmost end. How many people were in the camp? Estimates range from a few thousand to over ten thousand.

The crowded camp was noisy. The day before had been busy with much to do. Scouts reported during that day that the Bluecoat soldiers rode toward the camp from the east. Several old men leaders addressed the council, but it was Sitting Bull they wanted to hear. A Cheyenne warrior remembered later, "There was only one who was considered as being above all others. This was Sitting Bull. He was recognized as the one old man chief of all the camps combined."

As to the Bluecoats, Sitting Bull told the council, "We will talk to them. But if they want to fight we will let them have it, so everybody be prepared."

That night Sitting Bull made medicine too and during the night his aunt, Four Horns' wife, had died. For such an important woman to die was an omen. The Bluecoats would attack! And they'd all be rubbed out!

When Sitting Bull left his tipi that Sunday morning, the village was a hive of activity. Bronzed boys watered the horses, patiently leading the ponies back and forth between the herd and the river. Nearby children splashed and swam in the cold stream and a short distance away several dug wild turnips. His wives and mother fleshed buffalo hides. His children played nearby and the newborn twins stood propped on cradleboards beside the women.

Later he slipped into the tipi, ate from a kettle, and lay down again to nap.

Pop! Pop! Sitting Bull sat up, startled at the shooting. It came from the lower end, his end of the camp. The Bluecoats!

Two frightened young men burst into the lodge, shouting, "They are firing into the camp." The popping grew more rapid.

Soon, One Bull, his bodyguard and nephew, was at the lodge. Holding an old Hawken rifle out to Sitting Bull, One Bull gave it up for a war club and shield handed him by his uncle. Sitting Bull set the Hawken aside, turned to One Bull and grasping his nephew's shoulders, said, "You will take my place and go out and meet the soldiers that are attacking us."

He paused, then added, his voice strained, but distinct, "Parley with them, if you can. If they are willing, tell them I will talk peace with them."

Waving Sitting Bull's shield in the air, One Bull raced off towards the charging Bluecoats, the area where the Bluecoat chief called Reno was attacking.

Sitting Bull picked up the Hawken and took the rein of his stallion, threw it over the shiny, black-maned neck of the animal and mounted. Where was his mother? The old woman moved around so slowly. Where was she? The Bluecoat soldiers might soon be in the camp racing through the tipis, rubbing out the women and children as they had on the Washita and at Sand Creek. Where his mother and wives fleshed the hides earlier, there was no one. Only staked-out skins.

Wheeling the stallion, Sitting Bull darted through the tipis. Women and children ran about in bunches, confused. Nowhere did he see his mother, children, or wives. He remembered later, "The squaws were like flying birds; the bullets were like humming bees."

Women screamed; children cried. Old men yelled with broken voices at the young men, urging them to hurry and meet the attack. The horses were running away! Sitting Bull struggled to weave his stallion through the warriors and their charging ponies, all rushing

*Sitting Bull at Fort Yates, Standing Rock Reservation. (Courtesy of Western History Collections, University of Oklahoma Library.)*

toward the Bluecoats at the lower end of the camp. Someone yelled, "The chargers are coming! They are charging! The chargers are coming!"

Where were they? His wives and mother? The children?

In the distance the guns popped. Clouds of dust drifted through the camp, chasing ponies and warriors rushing to the fight. The popping guns rang in Sitting Bull's ears. It was a bad fight.

As the dust around him cleared, he saw a great rush of people on foot headed away from the fighting toward the benchland to the west. Prodding his stallion, Sitting Bull galloped through the short grass after them. When he caught up, he called out to several of the women. His family, where were they? They pointed him ahead, up the slope.

The big stallion charged off toward the slope and soon he saw his wives, Four Times and Seen By Her Nation. The children were there; his mother walked a short distance behind the others. He spoke to them, but only briefly, then galloped back to where the Bluecoats were attacking.

The Bluecoats pressed closer! They were everywhere! (Sitting Bull feared more than ever for the camp's safety. Just over a year later, a reporter asked if he thought the Bluecoats would win. He answered, "There was so much doubt about it that I started down there to tell the squaws to pack up the lodges and get ready to move away.")

But then, from the lower end of the camp, a young man burst out of the dust, riding straight toward him. The rider smiled through dust and sweat. Over the noise of the battle, he yelled, "No use to leave camp; every white man is killed."

Still, the smoke and dust boiled. More riders came straight at him. They were Cheyenne and Oglala Sioux. They had stopped the Bluecoats! There was little doubt! The Bluecoats were running back to the Greasy Grass! The popping of the guns and the shrill whistles of the charging Hunkpapa faded. He rode back to where the women and children waited.

Nearly all of the warriors at the Hunkpapa end, the lower end of the camp, now passed toward the head of the village. Some of the Bluecoat pack mules ran loose. The young men chased them. Hundreds of warriors swarmed down the valley now. Sitting Bull watched from the benches. Women, children and old men crowded around him. The dust began to rise on the ridge across the valley. The women were singing and cheering the warriors on. Dogs barked and young boys strained to hold spare ponies and keep sight of the battle area. But there was nothing to see. A great cloud of billowing dust and gunsmoke shrouded the entire ridge above the hundreds of tipis.

Still the guns popped, shots so close together they sounded like canvas ripping. Out of the cloud of dust and smoke, riderless horses charged, stampeding away from the confusion. But the killing did not last long. And as the dust and smoke began to settle, Sitting Bull rode the black stallion at a trot toward the battlefield. The women poured down off the benches after him. Several exhausted warriors passed by without a word. Then Sitting Bull met another group. He asked quietly, "Are they all killed?"

"Yes," one among them answered, his head bowed.

*Short Woman, Sitting Bull's sister. (Courtesy of the Bureau of American Ethnology, Smithsonian Institution.)*

A sad smile crossed Sitting Bull's face. It was done. The Bluecoats were all rubbed out! He rasped, his voice almost a whisper, "Let's go back to camp."

If the battle of the Little Bighorn that hot, sunny day was Custer's Last Stand, then it too was Sitting Bull's.

Various people met and studied Sitting Bull during these years. A news correspondent, John F. Finerty, described him: "His hair, parted in the ordinary Sioux fashion, was without a plume. His broad face, with a prominent hooked nose and wide jaws, was destitute of paint. His fierce, half-bloodshot eyes gleamed from under brows which displayed large perceptive organs, and, as he sat there on his horse regarding me with a look which seemed blended of curiosity and insolence, I did not need to be told that he was Sitting Bull."

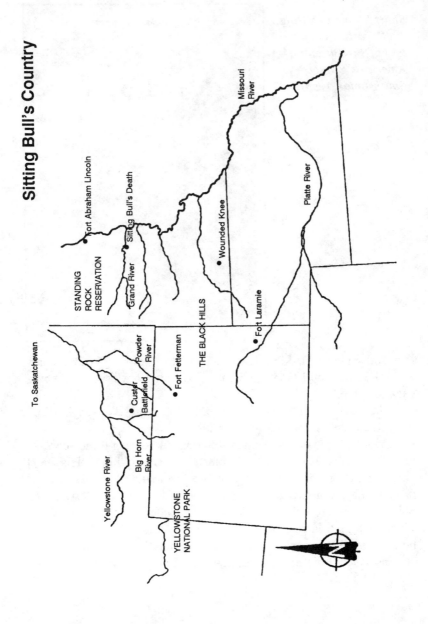

Sitting Bull's Country

Captain Walter Clifford, U.S. Army, wrote, "Sitting Bull does not strike one at first sight as an intellectual man but a little study reveals deep character in every line of his face."

An Army scout named Fred M. Hans met Sitting Bull about 1879 and wrote, "Sitting Bull is a medium built Indian about 5 ft. 8 or 9 inches tall; Weight about 170; About 50 years old; Small cunning black eyes & of a conservative disposition. I should credit him as being somewhat above average of his race for intelligence."

An Indian agent, James McLaughlin, who disliked Sitting Bull, admitted, "He had no single quality that would serve to draw his people to him, yet he was by far the most influential man of his nation for many years."

Never considered to be a chief by his own people, he was a medicine man. Or as he once said, "Just a man." Iron Hail (called Dewey Beard), an Oglala Sioux, remembered Sitting Bull. Iron Hail said, "We all rallied around him because he stood for our old way of life and the freedom we had always known."

Sitting Bull told reporters once that he was born on Willow Creek in South Dakota near Old Fort George during the same year Thunder Hawk was born. That would have made him 37 or 38 years old at the time of the Custer Fight. Others claim, among them his mother, that he was born about 1831.

Sitting Bull's band of Sioux, the Hunkpapa, "the people who camp alone," were one of several groups that belonged to the western-most Teton division of the Sioux people.

Like most Sioux youth, Sitting Bull had several names. From birth most called him Hunkeshnee, or "Slow." One account calls him Sacred Standshoty from about age ten until he counted coup by bravely touching an enemy, a dead Crow Indian, with a stick at age fourteen. Then he was given a name which Sioux Indians claim meant "A Buffalo Bull Resides Permanently Among Us," and shortened by whites to Sitting Bull.

It was 1863 when Sitting Bull first faced the Bluecoats. And in 1864 at Killdeer Mountain, he fought the Bluecoats. In 1865, the Oglala Sioux leader Red Cloud asked all people to help protect the Powder River Country of Wyoming. Whites had found gold and wanted to

*A drawing by Sitting Bull. It depicts Sitting Bull on the horse, counting coup by striking an enemy. (Courtesy of the Bureau of American Ethnology, Smithsonian Institution.)*

build a big road to Montana. Red Cloud warned, "The home of the people is to be taken from us. I prefer to die fighting rather than by starvation."

After Red Cloud, Sitting Bull and Crazy Horse, the Oglala war chief, fought the Bluecoats in the Battle of the Hundred Slain, the fight whites called the Fetterman Massacre, U.S. President Andrew Johnson negotiated a treaty with Red Cloud. General William T. Sherman came to Fort Laramie and the pact was called the Sherman Treaty or the Treaty of Laramie. That was during 1868.

As Sitting Bull saw it, the treaty was not a good one since it set boundaries, allowing whites to surround his people. He said, "The white people have put bad medicine over Red Cloud's eyes to make him see everything and anything they please." Sitting Bull refused to sign the treaty.

Not long after, Red Cloud realized his mistake. "The whites, who are educated and civilized, swindled me, and I am not hard to swindle, because I do not know how to read and write." When Sitting Bull heard this, he shrugged and exclaimed, "Well, what did he expect?"

These treaties talked of reservations and Sitting Bull opposed that life. He said once, "I don't want anything to do with a people who make a brave carry water on his shoulders, or haul manure." On another occasion, he admonished others who took reservation rations, "You are fools to make yourselves slaves to a piece of bacon fat, some hardtack, and a little sugar and coffee."

By 1874, when Custer found gold in the Black Hills of South Dakota, the whites began pouring in, violating the 1868 treaty. U.S. President Ulysses S. Grant tried to buy the Black Hills. When a special messenger to Sitting Bull's camp explained the deal, Sitting Bull responded, "I want you to go tell the Great Father that I do not want to sell any land to the government." Holding up a pinch of dirt, he added, "Not even as much as this."

In the fall of 1875, with many or the Sioux and Cheyenne peoples hunting off the reservations, the United States declared that all "wild and lawless bands" off the reservation were hostile and sent the Bluecoat soldiers to punish them.

Early in 1876, others left the reservations. Sitting Bull, by his ways, seems to have set an example that many of these people who wished to hunt and remain free followed. Years later, a Cheyenne named Wooden Leg who was in the big camp on the Little Bighorn, praised Sitting Bull: "I have no ears for hearing anybody say he was not a brave man. He had a big brain and a good one, a strong heart and a generous one. In the old times I never heard of any Indian having spoken otherwise of him."

Meanwhile the United States had sent soldiers to find the Indians. On June 17, 1876, warriors from the big camp fought General George Crook to a standstill on Rosebud Creek. They then eliminated the Bluecoat chief the Cheyenne called Squaw-Killer Custer on June 25. But it was just a battle; the war did not end. Sitting Bull said at the time, "Now the soldiers will give us no rest."

And he was right. For the next eleven months, there was time only to stay away from the Bluecoats. The large camp on the Little Bighorn did not stay together. Too many people together needed too much grass for the ponies, too much wood for the fires, and too much game for the people. So they broke into their normal small bands and scattered throughout Wyoming, Montana and the Dakotas to try and save the lives of the women, the children and the old men.

And chasing the Sioux people were General Crook and 2,100 soldiers, General Alfred Terry and 1,600 more, and Colonel Nelson Miles and his soldiers.

They caught up with American Horse's people in September, Sitting Bull's people in October, Dull Knife's people in November, Crazy Horse's people in January, 1877, and Lame Deer's people in May, 1877.

In Sitting Bull's case, he slipped away and by May, 1877, Sitting Bull's camp of about 135 lodges slipped across the Medicine Line to Canada to present-day Saskatchewan.

Sitting Bull's people were welcomed by Northwest Mounted Police Major James M. Walsh at Pinto Buttes just twenty-five miles or so into Canada. The red-coated Walsh explained Northwest Territorial law and Sitting Bull replied, "Yesterday, I was fleeing from white men, cursing them as I went. Today, the White Forehead Chief (Walsh) walks to my lodge alone and unarmed. He gives me the hand of peace." Thus began a friendship that lasted through both men's lifetimes.

Beginning that year, Americans came north to try to convince Sitting Bull to return to a reservation in the United States. General Alfred Terry was one of the first to ask. Priests of the Catholic Church, Father Martin Marty and Father Jean Baptiste Genin both tried to convince Sitting Bull. Always, except in isolated cases where he crossed the border briefly to hunt, he refused, happy in Canada away from the dreaded Bluecoats.

But by 1880, the food shortage was critical. The oldest enemy, starvation, became a daily problem. The Americans were killing all the buffalo. The large herds no longer ranged as far north as Canada. Suddenly, the only thing that mattered was survival. Sitting Bull said,

"The sufferings of my people makes my heart weak. Those who wish to go back may do so; I will place nothing in their way." And the stream of migration began again, this time southward, back to the land of Bluecoats and fear.

Still determined to help his people in a last effort, Sitting Bull turned to his friend Major Walsh during the summer of 1880 and said, "If the White Mother (Queen Victoria) is determined to drive me out of her country and force me into the hands of those who are waiting for me like hungry wolves, I beg you to see the White Father (President Rutherford Hayes) and find out the best conditions upon which I can return; also if the conditions will be faithfully and fully carried out."

The Canadian government, unwilling to rankle the Americans, replaced Walsh and refused pleas from Sitting Bull for aid. Still he pleaded, saying, "I shake hands with the White man on this side and I feel safe. I shake hands with the Americans and I am afraid of them."

His people continued fleeing south, trading hunger for the restricted life of an agency Indian. And finally, on July 19, 1881, about noon, Sitting Bull and 186 Hunkpapas rode into Fort Buford, Dakota Territory. Beside him, his large eyes staring from a hungry face, was his seven-year-old son Crowfoot.

The two were led to Major David H. Brotherton, Fort Buford's commander. Sitting Bull handed his son a Winchester Model 1866 Carbine and said to Brotherton, "I surrender this rifle to you through my son, whom I desire to teach in this manner that he has become a friend of the Americans. I wish it to be remembered that I was the last man of my tribe to surrender his rifle."

He told Brotherton, "I will fight no more. I do not love war. I never was the aggressor. I fought only to defend my women and children.

"I do not wish to be shut up in a corral. It is bad for young men to be fed by an agent. It makes them lazy and drunken. All agency Indians I have seen were worthless. They are neither wolf nor dog. But," he sighed, "my followers are weary of cold and hunger."

Promised amnesty if he would surrender, Sitting Bull and his family were instead imprisoned for two years at Fort Randall near present

Pickstown, South Dakota. The United States government explained, "It was considered best to give them a taste of military control."

During his stay at Fort Randall, Sitting Bull received Sioux visitors from throughout Indian country. "Fan mail" poured in from all over the world until the U.S. Army saw fit to appoint a Lieutenant Colonel George P. Ahern in charge of Sitting Bull's mail.

Then on May 10, 1883, Sitting Bull and his family were released to Standing Rock Reservation in the Dakotas. In the years that followed, Sitting Bull continued to oppose the Americans, but in a different way. He toured the East Coast, making speeches about how all the buffalo were killed and how fighting was no longer necessary and how he hoped his people could be educated. White translators said Sitting Bull was describing his bloody battles. They said his words were about the killing and the violent, savage life of a great Indian chief. Once, in 1884, while touring with Colonel Alvaren Allen, in Philadelphia, he was billed as "the murderer of Custer." His speech was one of friendship and peace. The interpreter's words incited the crowd to hiss at the old man.

In 1885 Buffalo Bill Cody used Sitting Bull to draw great crowds to his Wild West Show. But Sitting Bull was a good student and learned much from his travels among white Americans. He said of Americans once, "Strangely enough, they have a mind to till the soil, and the love of possession is a disease with them. These people have made many rules that the rich may break, but the poor may not; they have a religion which the poor worship, but the rich will not. They take tithes from the poor and weak to support the rich and those who rule."

He observed carefully and said, "They claim this mother of ours, the Earth, for their own use, and fence their neighbors away from her, and deface her with their buildings and their refuse. They compel her to produce out of season, and when sterile she is made to take medicine in order to produce again. All this is sacrilege."

Annie Oakley, also with the Cody show that year, claimed Sitting Bull gave most of the money he made to "small, ragged boys." She claimed Sitting Bull put little faith in men who let their own flesh and blood go hungry.

And when Sitting Bull had seen enough, he returned to his people where he could work to preserve what was left. He built a log cabin, raised chickens and cattle, farmed a little, and saw to it that his children went to school at a day school built nearby. Throughout the 1880's, the U.S. Congress tried to reduce the size of the reservations, once offering eight cents an acre for much of it. Most attempts fell short, but in 1889, over the protests of Sitting Bull, a commission led by General George Crook succeeded in getting many of the Sioux to agree.

When a newspaperman asked Sitting Bull what the Indians thought about their reservations being broken up, he replied, disgusted, "Indians! There are no Indians left but me!" After the commission left, promised payment did not come and rations were cut by twenty percent. Times again became desperate. In just twenty-five short years, the Sioux nation's hunting grounds and way of life were whittled down to a worthless patch of ground. Their buffalo were dead; their lives were turned upside down.

It was these conditions, then, that led a Brule Sioux called Short Bull, a Minneconjou Sioux named Kicking Bear and nine other Sioux leaders to travel to Nevada to visit Wovoka, a Paiute messiah who claimed to have a message for all tribes, a message given him by God.

The message, which came to be called the Ghost Dance religion, was non-violent and promised that since Christ had come as a white man and was crucified, he would return as an Indian. Dead ancestors, buffalo and the old ways would return too. All the Indians had to do was sing and dance the special way Wovoka explained. While they danced, they'd wear special ghost shirts that no white man's bullet could penetrate.

With this Ghost Dance religion also came new hope for a people who had little, a new promise for a people who knew only lies, a new future for a people who felt they had none.

The Americans, the whites living on and near the reservations, looked at it all differently. They feared the Indians planned a new uprising. And in October 1890, the Indian Bureau called for the hated and feared Bluecoats. They wanted the soldiers to return to the reservations to watch the Indians.

At Standing Rock, the agent, James McLaughlin, claimed Sitting Bull was causing the "disturbance" and demanded he be arrested. Both the Commissioner of Indian Affairs and Secretary of War disagreed, warning that the arrest could only bring more trouble.

A short time later, however, a list of "trouble-makers" was requested by the commander of the Army of the Dakotas, General Nelson A. Miles. On that list was Sitting Bull's name and Miles asked Sitting Bull's friend Buffalo Bill Cody to make the arrest. Miles told Cody, "Sitting Bull might listen to you when under the same conditions he'd take a shot at one of my soldiers."

McLaughlin apparently delayed Cody and had the orders changed to allow his Indian police to make the arrest just before dawn on December 15, 1890.

Forty-three Sioux policemen backed by a squadron of U.S. Cavalry rode carefully among the cabins on the Grand River where Sitting Bull, his wives, mother and daughter all lived. Nearby was a stable and corral. A small henhouse stood in the tiny settlement. Lieutenant Henry Bull Head of the Indian police dismounted and rapped on Sitting Bull's door and was told to come in.

Sitting Bull sat up, naked, lit a lamp and heard the dark figures in the doorway proclaim, "I come after you to take you to the agency. You are under arrest."

There was no argument. Sitting Bull merely said, "Let me put on my clothes and go with you." But then over the next few minutes conditions changed. The police became nervous as a crowd of over a hundred gathered outside the door.

Catch-the-Bear, a friend and bodyguard to Sitting Bull, came up just as Sitting Bull and the police stepped out of the cabin into the dark. Catch-the-Bear yelled, "You think you are going to take him. You shall not do it."

Lieutenant Bull Head sensed his position, then said calmly to Sitting Bull, "Come now, do not listen to anyone." And Bull Head and Red Tomahawk pushed Sitting Bull, moving him through the crowd.

That was enough for Catch-the-Bear. He threw off his blanket and in the same instant jerked off a shot from his rifle, striking Bull Head in the side.

Policeman Red Tomahawk followed behind Sitting Bull. He held his pistol drawn and poked into the small of Sitting Bull's back. As Lieutenant Bull Head fell, he fired a shot that tore upward into Sitting Bull's chest. Red Tomahawk reacted to Bull Head's shot an instant later by jerking the trigger of his big pistol, sending a bullet into Sitting Bull's head. Sitting Bull died instantly.

Suddenly everything was crazy. Sitting Bull's people lashed out at the police with clubs and guns, firing wildly, crying out angrily in their grief. Inside the cabin, the police found Sitting Bull's son, 17-year-old Crowfoot.

They executed him. Outside, the madness continued until the cavalry squadron began lobbing Hotchkiss shells into the area. Then Sitting Bull's people retreated, leaving six policemen and eight Indians, including Sitting Bull, dead.

But the killing was not done. Everywhere, those people who heard of the killing of Sitting Bull feared the worst. The Bluecoat soldiers would come shooting now and kill them all.

One band of people, the Minneconjous of an old man named Big Foot, fled toward Pine Ridge Reservation in hopes his people would be safe there. But on a bitter, cold December 28, Big Foot's people met four troops of the U.S. Seventh Cavalry.

Big Foot flew a white flag over his wagon. He didn't want to fight. After a short discussion in which Big Foot explained his destination, Major Samuel Whitside ordered Big Foot and his people to a cavalry camp at Wounded Knee Creek.

The 120 Sioux men and 230 Sioux women and children received rations, some extra tents and made camp in the middle of two troops of cavalry, under the watchful eyes of two Hotchkiss guns on a rise overlooking the rows of tipis. (In the night, more units of the Seventh arrived and placed two more Hotchkiss guns on the rise.)

The next morning, the Bluecoats, all of them, surrounded the camp. Big Foot's people were told to give up their weapons and they did, but the Bluecoat chief, Colonel James W. Forsyth, said there were more and sent soldiers to rummage through the tipis.

Fear, mistrust, disbelief and anger were all present and a short time later, while attempting to disarm a young deaf Minneconjou

*Big Foot, the old leader of the Minniconjou Sioux, was sick and spitting blood when the Seventh Cavalry escorted him to Wounded Knee in 1890. He is dead in this picture.*

named Black Coyote, the young man's rifle accidently discharged. That was the fatal beginning of rapid firing by a half dozen young Indian men and a contingent from the nearly five hundred men and officers of the U.S. Seventh Cavalry, Custer's old outfit. Adding to the confusion, the four Hotchkiss guns sprayed the area, firing about fifty two-and-one-half pound shells a minute among Big Foot's people, the shrapnel from the bursts tearing and ripping human and horse flesh alike.

Finally, when it ended, there were at least 153 of Big Foot's people dead. Some estimate that as many as three hundred of his folk were killed in the shooting, their bodies scattered for miles around the peaceful Christian mission church that stood a couple hundred yards northwest of the battle site.

The Seventh Cavalry counted 25 dead, 39 wounded, most victims of their own bullets, their own shrapnel.

A blizzard swept Wounded Knee that afternoon and it was several days before the frozen corpses of Big Foot and his people were collected and dumped into a mass grave that is marked today by a monument at Wounded Knee, South Dakota.

In the meantime, on Standing Rock Reservation, they stuffed Sitting Bull into a wooden coffin, loaded him on a wagon and delivered the body to Fort Yates. Just at the edge of the agency town, they buried the body and marked it with a crude monument.

Today Fort Yates is located in North Dakota and Standing Rock Reservation extends south into South Dakota and includes Sitting Bull's Grand River home where he lived and died. In April 1953, someone removed Sitting Bull's remains and moved them south to a point about ten miles southwest of Mobridge, South Dakota. Not far from the Missouri River on a little-used road, a monument marks the grave.

Much has been written about Sitting Bull in nearly a century since his tragic death, but Major James Morrow Walsh of the Northwest Mounted Police knew Sitting Bull as well as any white man. He wrote of his friend, Bull:

"History does not tell us that a greater Indian than Bull ever lived—he was the Mohammed of his people—the law-giver and King of the Sioux."

# 7    Comanche: The Survivor

The popping guns grew silent. The great cloud of dust and gunsmoke that moments earlier shrouded the hillside began to clear and settled.

The young Sioux and Cheyenne men looked around, wild-eyed at all the death. Blue-coated troopers lay sprawled grotesquely, the life ripped quickly from them, leaving faces full of pain, full of fear.

Down by the river, the Little Bighorn, screams of joy broke the silence. Women and children rushed back into the camp, safe now from these Bluecoats that wanted to kill them all. Instead, the Bluecoats died.

In the hours that followed, there was much to do. Many of the Cheyenne women went among the dead Bluecoats, stripping and mutilating the bodies. It was the custom. Some dropped their tipis, moving them away from this death. This too was custom. Others collected the Bluecoat horses that the young men had gathered and driven to the river. The horses were thirsty and while they drank from the Little Bighorn, the women easily caught them.

The next day, June 26, as the sun fell toward the mountains, the Sioux-Cheyenne camp and the Bluecoat horses moved away from the great battle site. Their scouts reported many more Bluecoats coming toward them from the north.

It was early on the morning of June 28, 1876, when Major Reno's surviving soldiers and General Terry's and Colonel Gibbon's men went to the Custer Battlefield to see to the dead. And there in the new dawn, brave men cried.

As the day wore on, the sun beat down on their tanned faces and the sweat and tears streaked their beards. The stench of the mutilated corpses and dead horses caused many to hold neckerchiefs to their nostrils as they walked over the battlefield.

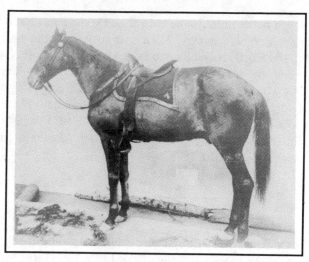

*Comanche, on display in a glass case at the University of Kansas at Lawrence.*

The U.S. military forces of General Alfred Howe Terry and Colonel John Gibbon had rendezvoused on the Little Bighorn as planned. Custer was a day early. The living, Terry and Gibbon's men and some of Reno's, were now going among the dead, Custer's men, and digging pits and burying the results of Custer's error. Here and there lay Army horses too. Most estimates put the dead cavalry mounts at seventy in the area of the Custer Fight.

Trooper Gustave Korn, a blacksmith, was one of the living on Wednesday, June 28, 1876. It was Trooper Korn that found what was thought to be "the only living representative of the bloody tragedy of the Little Bighorn, Montana, June 25, 1876"—Comanche. (There were others who claimed over the years that they'd discovered Comanche on the battlefield. Among them was regimental quartermaster Lieutenant Henry J. Nowlan.)

Comanche, Captain Myles Keough's 15-hand-high bay gelding, was found lying where Keogh and I Company had fallen. Comanche raised his head and neighed. The gelding dripped blood, red blotches seemed to almost cover his coat. He could hardly stand or walk. They counted seven bullet holes in the animal and some considered it best to put him out of his misery. Korn saw to it that the horse was returned to the *Far West* and then to Fort Abraham Lincoln. Over the next few weeks the severely wounded horse received the attention he needed. His wounds mended slowly and he was finally assigned, by General Order No. 7, on April 10, 1878, to a permanent place in the hearts of I Company, Seventh Cavalry:

"Headquarters Seventh U.S. Cavalry, Fort Abraham Lincoln, Dakota Territory, April 10, 1878.

---

**General Orders No. 7:**

1. The horse known as 'Comanche,' being the only living representative of the bloody tragedy of the Little Big Horn, Montana, June 25, 1876, his kind treatment and comfort should be a matter of special pride and solicitude on the part of the 7th Cavalry, to the end that his life may be prolonged to the utmost limit. Though wounded and scarred, his very silence speaks in terms more eloquent than words of the desperate struggle against overwhelming numbers, of the hopeless conflict, and heroic manner in which all went down that day.
2. The commanding officer of I Troop will see that a special and comfortable stall is fitted up for Comanche; he will not be ridden by any person whatever under any circumstances, nor will he be put to any kind of work.
3. Hereafter upon all occasions of ceremony (of mounted regimental formation), Comanche, saddled, bridled, and draped in mourning, and led by a mounted trooper of Troop I, will be paraded with the regiment.

By command of Colonel Sturgis:
    (signed) E.A. Garlington,
    1st Lieutenant and Adjutant, 7th U.S. Cavalry."

Along with other horses, the Army had purchased Comanche in the spring of 1868 at St. Louis. The Seventh Cavalry was in camp near

*This pictograph, done by Red Horse in 1881, shows warriors leading American horses from the site of the Custer Fight. (Courtesy of the Bureau of American Ethnology, Smithsonian Institution.)*

Ellis, Kansas when the gelding joined the regiment. In September, 1868, on the Cimarron River, the horse was in action and wounded by a Comanche Indian. The wound and subsequent scar marked the horse that all came to call Comanche. Keogh was riding Comanche in that first incident also.

Gustave Korn continued to take care of the horse until Korn himself was killed at Wounded Knee on December 29, 1890. Comanche spent his last days at Fort Riley, Kansas and died there of colic, less than a year after Korn was killed, in November 1891. He was about 29 years old. Two years later, in 1893, Comanche stood on exhibit at the World's Fair in Chicago where he was viewed by hundreds of thousands of visitors. He had been mounted and stuffed by Professor L.L. Dyche at the University of Kansas.

Today, Comanche stands on display at the University of Kansas Museum of Natural History, the Dyche Museum, at Lawrence. A visitor sees the McClellan saddle cinched tightly over a U.S. 7th

Cavalry blanket. The "US" brand on Comanche's left shoulder appears as awesome as the long scar on his left hindquarter. Of the several wounds Comanche received, only three were severe — one on the hindquarter, another on the shoulder, and the third in the neck.

There have been a number of requests to move the display to other locations, some temporary requests, others for permanent removal. These have always been rejected. As a result, Comanche remains in his glass case on the campus of the University of Kansas.

Was Comanche truly the sole survivor of that famous battle? Too often the answer has been a firm and final: Yes!

But the Sioux and Cheyenne that rode away in front of Terry's column would naturally disagree, since they too were survivors. And, perhaps more interesting is that a number of Seventh Cavalry mounts survived the battle. Some say as many as 140 of Custer's men's mounts survived. The victors rode away on many of these survivors. Wooden Leg, Thomas Marquis' Cheyenne informant, remembered seeing a number of "soldier horses taken by the Indians." He said, "They were fat and sleek and strong and lively. They were better than any of the Indian horses."

On May 19, 1883 (St. Paul, *Minnesota Pioneer Press* ), Spotted-Horn-Bull told how a warrior had pursued a soldier and after the soldier committed suicide, the Sioux warrior caught his horse. Spotted-Horn-Bull concluded, "He had a good horse and the Sioux rode him for years after that."

Joseph White Cow Bull, an Oglala Sioux, remembered later, "The battle was over. Soon we were shouting victory yells. Then the women and children heard us, they came out on the ridge to strip the bodies and catch some of the big horses the soldiers had ridden."

On October 6, 1876, the *New York Herald* printed the story of a Sioux, Kill Eagle. In the interview, the Little Bighorn survivor said, "I saw lots of soldiers' horses."

Other horses were found alive. One trooper remembered finding a horse wounded in the back. He shot him to get him out of his misery. Lieutenant Edward Godfrey wrote in his diary three days after the battle, "I found a gray horse. I took him in." One of Reno's men found a horse called Billy, a light bay with four white feet, that lived around Cheyenne, Wyoming until his death in 1900, age 37. Others claimed a gray named Nap from E Company was returned to Fort Abraham Lincoln and was a children's pet there for several years. And there were other accounts. So obviously there were many horse-survival stories. But one of the more interesting accounts is that from the files of the North-West Mounted Police as cited in J.P. Turner's *The North-West Mounted Police, 1873–1893*.

After the Custer Fight, many of the Sioux under Sitting Bull headed toward Canada, Grandmother's Land, the Sioux called it. The Sioux crossed the border with four thousand U.S. soldiers hounding their trail, all seeking revenge.

In Canada, the Sioux were greeted by the North-West Mounted Police. The Red Coats were firm, but friendly, with the Sioux, and this treatment prompted a mutual respect interrupted by only rare hostile encounters between the Indians and the Police.

The Sioux brought with them the spoils of victory that only such an overwhelming defeat of an enemy could yield. There were Springfield carbines and U.S. Army handguns, U.S. Cavalry bridles and bits, and distinctive McClellan saddles. And too, the Sioux brought U.S. Seventh Cavalry horses.

In the two years, 1877-1879, that followed, one of the Sioux traded a grey horse to the Metis. (This survivor could have been from Lieutenant Algernon E. Smith's Grey Horse Troop, Company E, or possibly a grey ridden by the buglars of Custer's command.) These half-blood traders, the Metis, roamed the plains in Montana and southern Saskatchewan. Subsequently, the Metis owner was spotted with his horse by Major James Morrow Walsh, Superintendent in charge of the North-West Mounted Police detachment at Wood Mountain in southern Saskatchewan.

Major Walsh, during 1879, noticed the U.S. Seventh Cavalry brand on the 12-year-old grey and sensed the significance of the horse's past. He offered to buy the grey out of compassion and with the intention or returning the horse to the United States government.

Two years earlier in the fall of 1877, General Alfred Terry, Commander of the Department of Dakota, led a United States government commission to Wood Mountain in an attempt to gain the return

*Major James Walsh, North-West Mounted Police. (Courtesy of the Royal Canadian Mounted Police.)*

of Sitting Bull and his people to United States Territory. Superintendent Walsh met and conferred with Terry at that time. Now, in the spring of 1879, Major Walsh decided that he'd inform General Terry of his discovery and if the United States government wished, return the horse to its rightful owners.

Major Walsh, in a letter to General Terry, stated: "If your government or any officer of the 7th Cavalry wishes to have him I will hand him over, but of the many relics I have seen of the battle of the Little Big Horn, none have taken my fancy like this old trooper, and having been for years an admirer of gallant Custer, and having conversed with the principal chiefs who took part in that memorable battle, to be permitted to keep this old trooper, which has come so strangely into my hands, would be a great pleasure."

Major Walsh, who was handling the refugee Sioux in his land with such deftness and responsibility, applied the same compassion to the horse and awaited a reply from General Terry.

At the Department of Dakota Headquarters, General Terry received the letter, considered it and decided that its importance was beyond his authority. Besides, the Seventh Cavalry already had a "sole survivor." Terry passed the information on to Washington, D.C.

In the weeks that followed, Walsh waited. Would "the old trooper" stay with him or not? Finally, in correspondence from Washington, Major Walsh received the decision:

"I have the honour to inform you that the Secretary of War authorizes Major Walsh to keep the horse.
                    (Signed) E.D. Townsend, Adjutant-General"

The fate of this other survivor of Custer's Last Stand is not known. Superintendent Walsh stayed in the Canadian Northwest for another decade and finally left the North-West Mounted police in pursuit of the coal business in Winnipeg and later, Manitoba. Whether "the old trooper" stayed with him remains another of the mysteries of history surrounding the battle of the Little Bighorn.

# The Custer Fight

Terry and Gibbon's March

Custer Hill

Cheyennes

Brule Sioux

Little Bighorn River

Benches

Oglala Sioux

Sans Arc Sioux

Minneconjou Sioux

Medicine Tail Coulee

Hunkpapa Sioux

Benches

Custer's March

Reno Hill

Reno's first and second positions

N

Reno's March

# 8     The New York Times
## Reports the Custer Fight

On page one of the *New York Times* on July 7, 1876, there appeared several dispatches dealing with the Custer Fight. News traveled more slowly then, no news accounts appearing before July and the New York papers running the story for the first time on July 6.

Several of those articles follow, complete with misspelled words and, in some cases, inaccurate information. But the reader will find these contemporary accounts and observations informative and reflective of the era.

*New York Times,* Friday, July 7, 1876:

### The Little Horn Massacre

Latest Accounts of the Charge
A force of four thousand Indians in position attacked by less than four hundred troops—Opinions of leading army officers of the deed and its consequences—Feeling in the community over the disaster.

Special Dispatch to the New York Times
The dispatches giving an account of the slaughter of Gen. Custer's command, published in the *Times* of yesterday, are confirmed and supplemented by official reports from Gen. A.H. Terry, commanding the expedition. On June 25 Gen. Custer's command came upon the main camp of Sitting Bull, and at once

attacked it, charging the thickest part of it with five companies, Major Reno, with seven companies attacking on the other side. The soldiers were repulsed and a wholesale slaughter ensued. Gen. Custer, his brother, his nephew, and his brother-in-law were killed, and not one of his detachment escaped. The Indians surrounded Major Reno's command and held them in the hills during a whole day, but Gibbon's command came up and the Indians left. The number of killed is stated at 300 and the wounded at 31. Two hundred and seven men are said to have been buried in one place. The list of killed includes seventeen commissioned officers.

It is the opinion of Army officers in Chicago, Washington, and Philadelphia, including Gens. Sherman and Sheridan, that Gen. Custer was rashly imprudent to attack such a large number of Indians, Sitting Bull's force being 4,000 strong. Gen. Sherman thinks that the accounts of the disaster are exaggerated. The wounded soldiers are being conveyed to Fort Lincoln. Additional details are anxiously awaited throughout the country.

### Confirmation of the Disaster

Dispatches from Gen. Terry received at Sheridan's headquarters—Theories of the battle—Probably ten thousand Sioux in position—The attack condemned as rash by officers of experience—Disposition of the wounded.

Chicago, July 6. — At the headquarters of Lieut. Gen. Sheridan this morning, all was bustle and confusion over the reported massacre of Custer's command. Telegrams were being constantly received, but most of them were of a confidential nature and withheld from publication. It is known that the unfortunate command broke camp on the North Rosebud on June 22 for the purpose of proceeding in a direction which would bring it to the point named about the 25th, at which place a bloody fight is reported to have taken time. The following dispatch, the last received at head quarters in this city previous to the news of the massacre, confirms the accounts given to the extent of showing that Custer intended to go to that place.

Camp on the North Rosebud, June 21, 1876,
Lieut. Gen. P.H. Sheridan, Commanding
Military Division of the Missouri, Chicago:

No Indians have been met with as yet, but traces of large and recent camp have been discovered twenty or thirty miles up the Rosebud. Gibbon's column will move this morning, on the north side of the Yellowstone, for the mouth of the Big Horn, where it will be ferried across by the supply steamer and whence it will proceed to the mouth of the Little Horn, and so on. Custer will go up the Rosebud to-morrow with his whole regiment, and thence to the head-waters of the Little Horn, thence down the Little Horn.

A.H. Terry,
Brigadier General Commanding

A dispatch received at the quarters of Gen. Sheridan this morning at 11 o'clock confirms the first reports received. The dispatch states that the forces were falling back, and that the wounded had been sent to Fort Lincoln. No details were given, but the officers at headquarters regarded it as a full confirmation of the engagement reported. In reply to an inquiry as to whether the attack was made by Gen. Custer of his own accord, or under orders from the department, an answer was given that Custer made the charge of his own volition. A still later dispatch from Lieut. Kinzie, of the Seventh Cavalry, was received, asking that he be transferred from the department where he is now on duty to the scene of action. This is also regarded as another confirmation of the bloody massacre reported. Gen. Custer's family are at Fort Lincoln, to which point the wounded are being conveyed.

So far as an expression in regard to the wisdom of Gen. Custer's attack could be obtained at head-quarters, it was to the effect that Custer had been imprudent, to say the least. It is the opinion at head-quarters among those who are most familiar with the situation, that Custer struck Sitting Bull's main camp. Gen. Drum, of Sheridan's staff, is of opinion that Sitting Bull began concentrating his forces after the fight with Crook, and that no doubt, Custer dropped squarely into the midst of no less than ten thousand red devils and was literally torn to pieces. The movement made by Custer is censured to some extent at military headquarters in this city. The older officers say it was brought about by that foolish pride which so often results in the defeat of men. It seems that a few days before Gen. Terry had offered four additional companies to Custer, but that officer refused them.

The information at headquarters further is to the effect that Gen. Gibbon with his force was known to be moving up to Custer for the purpose of reinforcing him, and that he [Custer] knew of this, and knew that Gibbon would arrive by the following day after the engagement. I have it on as good authority as one of the leading officers at head quarters, that Custer had been ordered by Terry to make a march toward the Little Big Horn and to form a junction with a column of infantry that was moving diagonally across the country to the same point. The two columns were then to co-operate and make an attack. Instead of marching from twenty to thirty miles per day, as ordered, Custer made a forced march and reached the point of destination two or three days in advance of the infantry; then finding himself in front of the foe he foolishly attempted to cut his way through and punish the red devils.

### Dispatches from Gen. Terry

Particulars of the plan of the movement under Custer as agreed on before the march.

Special Dispatch to the *New York Times*

Philadelphia, July 6.—This afternoon Gen. Sheridan received two dispatches from Gen. Terry relative to the Indian battle in which Gen. Custer was killed, and this evening the telegrams were handed to your correspondent. Gen. Sherman says that he thinks the first dispatch giving the details of the battle was mislaid, or else some enterprising newspaper correspondent bought up the messenger and sent the account East, thus keeping the War Department in ignorance of the occurrence. From what he knows of the occurrence he believes that Gen. Custer attempted a battle without reconnoitering the position, and that he was too bold. He does not think the slaughter so great as at first reported. The first dispatch received by Gen. Sheridan was as follows:

Camp on Yellowstone near Mouth of Big Horn, July 2.

On the evening of the 28th we commenced moving down with the wounded, but were able to get along but four miles as the hand litters did not answer the purpose. The mule litters did excellently well, but they were insufficient in number, therefore the 29th was spent in making a full supply of them. On the evening of the 29th we started again, and at 2 a.m. the wounded were placed on the steamer at the mouth of the Little Big Horn. The afternoon of the 30th they were brought down to the depot on the Yellowstone. I send them tomorrow by steam to Fort Lincoln, and with them one of my aids, Capt. E.W. Smith, who will be able to answer any questions which you may desire to ask. Col. Sheridan's dispatch informing me of the reported gathering of Indians on the Rosebud reached me after I came down here. I hear nothing of Gen. Crook's movements. At least a hundred horses are needed to remount the cavalrymen now here.

 (Signed) Alfred H. Terry,
      Brigadier General

The second dispatch was as follows:

Camp Big Horn, July 2.

I think I owe it to myself to put you more fully in possession of the facts of the late operations. While at the mouth of the Rosebud I submitted my plan to Gen. Gibbon and Gen. Custer. It was that Custer, with his whole regiment, should move up the Rosebud till he should meet a trail Reno had discovered a few days before, but that he should not follow it directly to the Little Big Horn, that he should send scouts over it and keep his main force further toward the south, so as to prevent the Indians from slipping in between himself and the mountains. He was also to examine the head waters of the Tollaska Creek, as he passed it, and send me word of what he found there. A scout was furnished him for the purpose of crossing the country to me. We calculated it would take Gibbons' column until the 26th to reach the mouth of the Little Big Horn, and that the wide sweep I had proposed Custer should make would require so much time that Gibbon would be able to cooperate with him in attacking any Indians that might be found on the stream. I asked Custer how long his marches would be. He said they would be at the rate of about thirty miles a day. Measurements were made and calculations based on that rate of progress. I talked with him about his strength and at the time suggested that perhaps it would be well for me to take Gibbon's cavalry and go with him. To the latter suggestion, he replied, "That, without reference to the command, he would prefer his own regiment alone. As a homogenous body, as much could be done with it as with the two combined. He expressed the utmost confidence that he had all the force that he could need, and I shared his confidence. The plan adopted was the only one which promised to bring the infantry into action, and I desired to make sure of things by getting up every available man. I offered Custer the battery of Gatling guns, but he declined it, saying that it might embarrass him, and that he was strong enough without it.

The movements proposed by Gen. Gibbon's column were carried out to the letter, and had the attack been deferred until it was up, I cannot doubt, that he should have been successful. The Indians had evidently prepared themselves for a stand, but as I learned from Capt. Benton that on the 22d the cavalry marched twelve miles, on the 23d, twenty-five miles; from 5 a.m. till 8 p.m., of the 24th, forty-five miles, and then after night ten miles further, resting, but without unsaddling, twenty-three miles, to the battlefield. The proposed route was not taken, but as soon as the trail was struck it was followed. I cannot learn that any examination of Tallaska Creek was made. I do not tell you this to cast any reflections upon Custer, for whatever errors he may have committed Custer's action is unexplainable in the case.

A.H. Terry, Brigadier General.

These dispatches were all that either Gens. Sherman or Sheridan received up to midnight, and were sent to the Secretary of War.

### Details of the Battle

Graphic description of the fighting—Major Reno's command under fire for two days—Every man of Custer's detachment killed except one scout—Affecting scenes when relief arrived.

Special Dispatch to the *New York Times.*
Chicago, July 6—A special to the *Times* tonight from Bismarck recounts most graphically the late encounter with the Indians on the Little Big Horn. Gen. Custer left the Rosebud on June 22, with twelve companies of the Seventh Cavalry, striking a trail where Reno left it, leading in the direction of the Little Horn. On the evening of the 24th fresh trails were reported, and on the morning of the 25th an Indian village, twenty miles above

the mouth of the Little Horn was reported about three miles long and half a mile wide and fifteen miles away. Custer pushed his command rapidly through. They had made a march of seventy-eight miles in twenty-four hours preceding the battle. When near the village it was discovered that the Indians were moving in hot haste as if retreating. Reno, with seven companies of the Seventh Cavalry, was ordered to the left to attack the village at its head, while Custer, with five companies, went to the right and commenced a vigorous attack. Reno felt of them with three companies of cavalry, and was almost instantly surrounded, and after one hour or more of vigorous fighting, during which he lost Lieuts. Hodgson and McIntosh and Dr. Dewolf and twelve men, with several Indian scouts killed and many wounded, he cut his way through to the river and gained a bluff 300 feet in height, where he intrenched and was soon joined by Capt. Benton with four companies. In the meantime the Indians resumed the attack, making repeated and desperate charges, which were repulsed with great slaughter to the Indians. They gained higher ground then Reno occupied, and as their arms were longer range and better than the cavalry's, they kept up a galling fire until nightfall. During the night Reno strengthened his position, and was prepared for another attack, which was made at daylight.

The day wore on. Reno had lost in killed and wounded a large portion of his command, forty odd having been killed before the bluff was reached, many of them in hand to hand conflict with the Indians, who outnumbered them ten to one, and his men had been without water for thirty-six hours. The suffering was heartrending. In this state of affairs they determined to reach the water at all hazards, and Col. Benton made a rally with his company, and routed the main body of the Indians who were guarding the approach to the river. The Indian sharpshooters were nearly opposite the mouth of the ravine through which the brave boys approached the river, but the attempt was made, and though one man was killed and seven wounded the water was gained and the command relieved.

When the fighting ceased for the night Reno further prepared for attacks.

There had been forty-eight hours' fighting, with no word from Custer. Twenty-four hours more of fighting and the suspense ended, when the Indians abandoned their village in great haste and confusion. Reno knew then that succor was near at hand. Gen. Terry, with Gibbon commanding his own infantry, had arrived, and as the comrades met men wept on each other's necks. Inquiries were then made for Custer, but none could tell where he was. Soon an officer came rushing into camp and related that he had found Custer, dead, stripped naked, but not mutilated, and near him his two brothers, Col. Tom and Boston Custer. His brother-in-law, Col. Calhoun, and his nephew Col. Yates, Col. Keuogh, Capt. Smith, Lieut. Crittenden, Lieut. Sturgis, Col. Cooke, Lieut. Porter, Lieut. Harrington, Dr. Lord, Mark Kellogg, the Bismarck Tribune correspondent, and 190 men and scouts. Custer went into battle with Companies C, L, I, F, and E, of the Seventh Cavalry, and the staff and non-commissioned staff of his regiment and a number of scouts, and only one Crow scout remained to tell the tale. All are dead. Custer was surrounded on every side by Indians, and horses fell as they fought on skirmish line or in line of battle. Custer was among the last who fell, but when his cheering voice was no longer heard, the Indians made easy work of the remainder. The bodies of all save the newspaper correspondent were stripped, and most of them were horribly mutilated. Custer's was not mutilated. He was shot through the body and through the head. The troops cared for the wounded and buried the dead, and returned to their base for supplies and instructions from the General of the Army.

Col. Smith arrived at Bismarck last night with thirty-five of the wounded. The Indians lost heavily in the battle. The Crow scout survived by hiding in a ravine. He believes the Indians lost more than the whites. The village numbered 1,800 lodges, and it is thought there were 4,000 warriors. Gen. Custer was directed to find and feel of the Indians, but not to fight unless Terry arrived with infantry and with Gibbon's column. The casualties foot up 261 killed and fifty-two wounded.

## The Scene of the Massacre

Description of the region by Major Grimes, who removed the forts in 1868 under the treaty.

Special Dispatch to the *New York Times*
St. Louis, July 6.—The news of the massacre of Gen. Custer with seventeen commissioned officers and 315 men, near the Little Big Horn River, has created an extraordinary sensation here. Subsequent advices received at military head-quarters in this city substantially confirm the terrible news. Your correspondent this evening had a conversation with Major J.M. Grimes, one of the military officers stationed here, and who is very familiar with Indian affairs in the West. He is well acquainted with the country where the fight took place. He was detailed by the Government in 1868 to remove all the forts on the Powder River route, in accordance with the provisions of the Fort Laramie treaty of 1868. The battle occurred about twenty miles from the mouth of the Little Big Horn River, which empties into the Big Horn, and the latter into the Yellow Stone. The fight took place on the Crow reservation, about forty miles east of Fort C.L. Smith, the most northern of the Powder River Road forts, removed by Major Grimes in 1868. The country is diversified by mountain ranges and deep canons, with intervening plateaus of sage brush prairies.

Ex-Gov. Fletcher, who was a member of the Peace Commission that went out last summer, stated to-night that the present desperate condition of affairs is only a legitimate result of the present peace policy pursued by the Government toward the Indians.

## The Causes and Consequences

Fruits of the ill-advised Black Hills Expedition of two years ago—Ability of the Army to renew operations effectively discussed—The personnel of the charging party still undefined.

Special Dispatch to the *New York Times*
Washington, July 6.—The news of the fatal charge of Gen. Custer and his command against the Sioux Indians has caused great excitement in Washington, particularly among Army people and about the Capitol. The first impulse was to doubt the report, or set it down as some heartless hoax or at least a greatly exaggerated story by some frightened fugitive. At the second thought the report was generally accepted as true in its chief and appalling incidents. The campaign against the wild Sioux was undertaken under disadvantageous circumstances owing to the refusal of Congress to appropriate money for the establishment of military posts on the upper Yellowstone River. Gen. Sherman and Gen. Sheridan both asked for these posts, which, in case of anticipated troubles would give the troops a base of supplies about four hundred miles nearer the hostile country than they could otherwise have. The posts desired would have been accessible by steam-boats on the Yellowstone, which would have conveyed men and supplies. The House Committee on Military Affairs unanimously recommended their establishment, but the Committee on Appropriations refused to provide in their bills the necessary means. This is regarded as the immediate cause of the disaster. The remote cause was undoubtedly the expedition into the Black Hills two years ago in violation of laws and treaties, authorized by Secretary Belknap and led by Gen. Custer. If there had been a post at the head or navigation on the Yellowstone the expedition would doubtless have proceeded thence against the Indians in one invincible column. The policy of sending three converging columns so many hundred miles against such brave and skillful soldiers as the Sioux has been the cause of some uneasiness here among

the few who have taken the trouble to think abut the facts and prospects. The Sioux seem to have understood clearly the plan of attack, and threw themselves with their whole force first against Gen. Crook's column and now against Custer's, and both times inflicted serious disaster. The feeling was common to-day that the campaign is a failure, and that there must follow a general Indian war, promising to be costly in men and money. The Sioux are a distinct race of men from the so-called Indians of the South-west, among whom the army found such easy work two or three years ago. The Sioux live by the chase and feed chiefly upon flesh. The Southern Indians are farmers and eat fruits and vegetables, the latter are at their worst cruel, coward-ly robbers. The former are as much like the brave and war-like red men represented by the *Last of the Mohicans* as ever existed outside the covers of fiction and romance. The difference be-tween the foes in the North and Southwest seems not have been well counted upon, nor provided for, and formed, as it might, prudently, no restraint upon the reckless fatal charge of the 300. If the tale told by the courier Taylor is true, the charge has scarce a parallel in the history of civilized or savage warfare. The massacre of Major Dade and his command in the Florida war is alone comparable with it in American history. The reason for an expedition against the Indians this summer is not well un-derstood, nor has any satisfactory explanation been published. The wild Sioux had never been willing to live on the reservations marked out for them, and the understanding has been that they were to be whipped into submission, and compelled to live like Red Cloud and Spotted Tail, with their bands, about the Government agencies. The question of the policy and the right of the war will now be renewed and discussed, and, indeed, is discussed to-day. Those who believe in the policy of the exter-mination of the Indians, and think the speedier the better its ac-complishment, look upon the condition of war as inevitable, and are for pouring thousands of troops into the Indian country and giving them a terrible punishment. This class is small, even in the Army, where the policy of extermination is not popular save with a few high and restless officers. The invasion of the Black Hills has been condemned over and over again by the peace party, and there are very many who can truthfully say, "I told you so." From that unwarranted invasion the present difficulties have gradually sprung up, so that an expedition that originally cost a hundred thousand dollars perhaps, must lead to an expenditure of millions, which will advance civilization in no way, except by the destruction of the uncivilized. The Army, if the present campaign wholly fails, is in no condition to renew hostilities with sufficient force, and there is little reason to expect Congress will this session provide for an Indian war. Thus by force of circumstances a continuation of the war would probably be with the Government forces upon the defensive, protecting as far as possible agencies and settlements. There is another result that some hope for. It is the union of the three columns of troops and the delivery of a blow against the Indians that will place them at the mercy of the Army and compel them to sue for peace. The chances are, however, so far as the information now at hand may be relied on, that the Govern- ment forces are much too small in number, reduced as they are by two battles, to meet the powerful and exultant Sioux.

Until advised of the particular five companies of the Seventh Cavalry with which Custer charged the Sioux, with results so disastrous to his command, the War Department will not be able to furnish the list of casualties. From the dispatches printed to-day, based on the information furnished by Muggins Taylor, the scout, it is inferred that Capts. Thomas W. Custer and Myles Moylan, and Lieut. James Calhoun, of the Seventh Cavalry, and Lieut. A.B. Crittenden, of the Fourth Infantry, were among those killed. Capt. Custer was a brother of Gen. Custer, Calhoun was his brother-in-law, and Moylan was brother-in-law to Calhoun. Gen. Custer had but one brother in the Seventh Cavalry. The report that the General and his two brothers were killed doubtless arose from the relationship described between Custer, Calhoun, and Moylan. Crittenden was the son of Col. Crittenden, of the Seventeenth Infantry, and grandson of the late John J. Crittenden, of Kentucky. At his own request he was detailed for active service against the Indians and assigned to the Seventh Cavalry. The only dispatch received today at the War Department was one from Adjutant Gen. Crum, of Sheridan's staff, stating that Gen. Terry, telegraphed from camp on Long Horn River, under date of July 2, confirming the report of the fight on June 25 of the death of Gen. Custer. Terry's dispatches were sent to Sheridan at Chicago and forwarded from there to Philadelphia, where Gens. Sherman and Sheridan now are.

# Part II:

# The Westerners

# 9    The Westerners

The year 1876 was also an important time in the lives of other Westerners. For example, just a few weeks after the Custer Fight, James Butler "Wild Bill" Hickok, drifted into Deadwood, Dakota Territory, the Black Hills area Custer had opened to gold miners two years earlier. And Hickok died in 1876, there in Deadwood, during August.

Wyatt Earp hired on at Dodge City, Kansas during 1876 as a policeman. That was in May. He quit in September and, as Hickok had done a couple months earlier, headed for Deadwood in search of Custer's gold. Both Hickok and Earp were more interested in "mining" the gold from miners at the poker table.

Allan Pinkerton, in 1876, wished he could lay his hands on the James Gang. He was especially eager after Jesse, Frank, the Youngers and others struck the First National Bank of Northfield, Minnesota on Thursday afternoon, September 7, 1876.

Charles E. Boles, better known as Black Bart—the PO8, was plying his trade in California during 1876. In particular, he stopped a stage at Cottonwood Peak on June 2. Characteristically, he waved the menacing shotgun, but said little, using the same method he employed against Wells Fargo until 1883.

William Miner, later more popularly known as Old Bill Miner, cooled his heels during 1876. He was wondering where his career was headed while occupying a lonely cell in California's San Quentin Prison. He'd sit there four more years before returning to his trade—stage and train robberies.

Rowdy Joe Lowe? In 1876, Rowdy Joe was missing. On purpose. Whereabouts unknown. Oh, there were those who wondered where he was. They said so. Put up wanted posters and rewards that said as

*Buffalo hides awaiting shipment from Dodge City.*

much. But by 1876, Rowdy Joe had used up his welcome in many parts of the West. In some ways, 1876 was too late for Rowdy Joe Lowe.

And 1876 was too late for some other things as well. Henry Raymond, for example, had already participated in the central Plains Great Slaughter of buffalo. The Great Slaughter, according to most, ran from 1872–1875. Buffalo hunting, however, had made a lasting mark on the West, a mark that determined the direction of life for many Westerners in 1876.

# 10  Henry Raymond and the Buffalo

The American buffalo, or bison, was on the North American continent from at least before Christ was on earth. When the white man arrived on the Great Plains, he threw all that history aside and in about a century reduced the buffalo population from sixty million to perhaps twenty lonely buffalo.

There were four great herds, the Northern, the Republican, the Arkansas and the Texas, roaming the million and a half square miles of Great Plains from Canada to Texas and the Missouri River to the Rockies. Visitors to the West marveled at the numbers of buffalo they saw. One stunned traveler claimed the herd he observed was "a compact black mass, extending beyond farther than we could see and coming in unbroken masses from the rear. The quaking of the earth and the rumble of the torrent continued for a long time, many estimating the herd to be from four to eight miles long and of unknown width. Surely many, many thousands of those animals."

Others observed great herds. One wrote, "The world looked like one robe." Another commented that "the rush of galloping bodies sounds like Niagara."

In the early 1800s, a market for buffalo robes developed in the East, the robes being purchased or traded from Indians. Later, Easterners bought buffalo tongues packed in brine. But as Western expansion continued, the Indian became a sore spot with whites. Eventually, it was determined that as long as the buffalo was on the Plains, there would be Indians on the Plains. Frank H. Mayer, a buffalo hunter, once had it explained to him by an Army officer of high rank thusly, "Mayer, there's no two ways about it: either the buffalo or the Indian must go. Only when the Indian becomes absolutely dependent on us for his every need, will we be able to handle him. He's too independent with the buffalo. But if we kill the buffalo we conquer the Indian. It seems a more humane thing to kill the buffalo than the Indian, so the buffalo must go."

The buffalo hunters—some called them "runners" since there was little sport in shooting what many men considered "unquestionably the stupidest game animal in the world"—of the 1870s were generally after robes and tongues whether it was the government encouraging them or not. Their motives were money. If the Indian lost in the process, that was little concern of theirs.

Hides in 1871 sold for about $1.25 each. A buffalo tongue was worth 25 cents and some paid one cent per pound for the hindquarter. (Later on buffalo bones sold well. It took about 100 buffalo to make a ton of bones. Delivered to a railroad agent, they usually brought about $8 per ton. Shipped east, they were ground into fertilizer.) But things were changing. The demand for cattle hides for tanning in the winter of 1870 had been greater than the supply. Some companies decided to try buffalo hides. In particular, German tanners in Philadelphia tried the buffalo hides and found they made good leather that could be used for boots, shoes, belts and particularly belts for machines, Suddenly everyone wanted buffalo hides. Tanneries advertised by newspaper and leaflets across the Plains. They said they'd pay $2.25 for buffalo cows and $3.25 for large bulls.

In Kansas, the best year for killing buffalo was 1872. The *Wichita Eagle* of November 7, 1872, reported, "It is estimated that there is, south of the Arkansas and west of Wichita, from one to two thousand men shooting buffalo for their hides alone."

On December 26, 1872, the *Newton Kansan* carried a similar story, but added that the average hunter was "bringing down about fifteen buffalo daily. The hams are worth 1-1/2 to 2 cents a pound and the hides from $1.50 to $2.50 a piece."

The period from 1872–1875 is sometimes referred to as the time when The Great Slaughter took place. In those years in Kansas, the buffalo migration was good to terrible. In 1872, there were plenty of buffalo. The next year was all right, but not as good as 1872. And 1873 was bad. Most figured the buffalo were done in Kansas. Actually, it took until 1878 for the Southern herd to be wiped out completely.

The first year of the Great Slaughter, the winter of 1872–73, Robert Wright was in business at Dodge City with Charles Rath. Wright wrote later, "Charles Rath and I shipped over two hundred thousand buffalo hides the first winter the Atchison, Topeka, and Santa Fe Railroad reached Dodge City, and I think there were at least as many more shipped from there, besides two hundred cars of hind quarters and two cars of buffalo tongues."

In the 1872–74 period, some claim 3,158,730 buffalo were killed around Dodge City and that didn't include another 405,000 killed by nearby Indians.

Once the hunter was in the field, he shot the buffalo, normally from a stand. The hunter generally crept up on the windward side of the herd. If possible, he preferred a position above the herd and out of sight. He was concerned that the herd not get his scent, but also that the wind would carry the sound of his gun away from the herd. The buffalo, like most hooved animals, had bad eyesight. Some claimed they shot the leader, usually a cow. She'd go down and the others, confused, might run a few hundred feet and another seemed to be the leader. Then the shooter dropped another and another. Some reported seeing buffalo walk to downed buffalo and either sniff or lick the oozing blood, then begin peacefully grazing nearby.

Hunters used most of the rifles that existed during the 1867–1883 period. Buffalo Bill Cody, for example, favored a Springfield Model 1866 military rifle in killing 4,280 buffalo in eighteen months work for the Kansas Pacific Railroad during 1867 and 1868.

Remington had a rolling-block .44–90 that was called "The Buffalo Gun." The Ballard .45–70 was popular. Some hunters used a make of Henry or Spencer. Others swore by the Sharps. These rifles were "heavy-bore single-shot breech-loading rifles." The most popular was the Sharps .50 caliber, the Big Fifty. Some claimed it would kill dependably at 1,000 yards, which was probably not a very dependable claim. Western wag Ned Buntline commented that to shoot a buffalo at that distance, the shooter had better load the gun with rock salt so as to preserve the meat until the hunter could get to the dead animal.

A buffalo gun might cost a hundred or a hundred and fifty dollars without a scope. A 10-power, 20-power or 30-power scope was sometimes added. A tripod was handy to use when firing a 12-pound Sharps with a 32-inch barrel.

The next phase of the hunt required the hide to be removed from the dead animal. Far from a simple task, the buffalo bull was often nine feet long and weighed maybe 1,800 to 2,200 pounds. Cows were smaller, weighing 800 to 1,200 pounds, by most accounts. The skinning chore was accomplished with one or two men skinning, usually with a horse helping by steadily pulling on a rope attached to the buffalo's skin. A skinner then used knives to snip stuck skin as the horse did most of the work. A good skinner did all this in about five minutes.

The fresh hides were said to be green. The green hides were anchored, hair down, to the ground with small wooden pegs. This allowed them to dry for transporting back to a railroad shipping point.

The hunters, their methods and their guns were very good. On the southern Plains, the buffalo was soon exterminated. There were still buffalo in the northern Plains, but the Sioux Indians discouraged white hunters in that area. In addition, there were fewer trains to transport hides from that area.

Eventually, with the defeat of the Sioux in the late 1870s, and the coming of the Northern Pacific Railroad, hunters swarmed after the buffalo. By 1883, the northern herd was done. Estimates vary, but an Associated Press story in the late 1880's claimed there were four buffalo in Dakota, ten in Montana, and 26 in Wyoming. An 1887 count had 1,091 in North America, half in Canada and 256 in captivity. An 1897 story claimed there were only twenty buffalo left in the United States. They were in Yellowstone National Park. And a 1903 article reported 34 buffalo alive in the United States.

In the 1870s, buffalo attracted many men to the West, all kinds of men. One place these tough men collected was Dodge City, Kansas. And often there was trouble.

March 1873: The door of the frontier dance hall slammed open, a spray of kerosene light splashing the street just ahead of a man named Burns. Mr. Burns was running for his life. The night was his only refuge. Right behind Burns was big Tom Sherman, the owner of the dance hall. Sherman held a fistful of pistol, bringing it up just often enough to jerk a shot at the frightened, fleeing Burns he'd chased from his dance hall.

Then as the fire exploded from the muzzle again, Sherman hit his target, sending Burns reeling, then tumbling in the street.

Burns was hit but not dead, as several others, including the shooter, Tom Sherman, came running up to where Burns lay wounded in the street. Burns looked up at Sherman. He was thrashing about on the ground now, his arms and legs pumping, trying to get away from the certain death Sherman packed in his big fist.

Sherman was gasping for air as he looked at Burns and said to the others, "I'd better shoot him again, hadn't I, boys?"

Then he moved closer to the writhing Burns, lifted the revolver so that he held it steady in both hands, and without waiting for an answer, aimed at Burns' forehead and squeezed the trigger.

Sherman's aim was bad what with the terrorized Burns churning about in the dim light and Sherman's haste to hit his mark. Still, the bullet did its job, scrambling Burns' brains and hair all over the ground.

That was Dodge City, Kansas, the night of Wednesday, March 12, 1873. It was a tough town, a town that had thrived on the slaughter of buffalo and had witnessed the deaths of men. One resident that first year claimed Burns and twenty-four others were killed.

A young witness to the Sherman shooting was 25-year-old Henry Raymond. He'd arrived in Dodge City for the first time in mid-November 1872 to join his buffalo hunting brother. The trail to Dodge City had begun for Henry in Illinois.

On November 11, 1872, Henry Raymond, the youngest of four sons of Charles and Harriet Raymond of near Carlinville, Illinois, traveled to St. Louis. That night, he boarded a train to Kansas City, then on to Topeka. From Topeka, young Henry traveled southwest to Sedgwick, a small town just north of Wichita, The train arrived at night and the next morning, Henry hiked ten miles to Thomas Masterson's in Grant Township of Sedgwick County. Masterson, also from Illinois, was the father of famous Western lawman Bat Masterson.

On Friday, November 15, 1872, Henry walked back to Sedgwick, made his way to Newton, then caught a train to Dodge City to join his brother Theodore and Thomas Masterson's sons, Bat and Ed. They were hunting buffalo near Dodge City.

It was almost 7 a.m. on November 16 when Henry's train arrived in Dodge City. The town wasn't very old. They'd called it Buffalo City until the summer of 1872 when someone in the Post Office Department claimed there were too many "Buffalo" in Kansas and renamed the town to honor nearby Fort Dodge.

The sluggish, shallow Arkansas River slipped by south of town, full of quicksand and sandbars, an irritating trickle for men weaned on the Mississippi and Ohio rivers.

Through the heart of town ran the Atchison, Topeka & Santa Fe Railroad tracks, dividing the "respectable" businesses north of the tracks from the "evil" businesses south of the tracks. The tracks had arrived in August.

Henry L. Stitler, a government teamster, had built a low sod house on the site in 1871 and tent saloons sprang up immediately. They laid out streets and in the summer of 1872 when railroad workers arrived, there was a general store, three dance halls and six saloons.

Bat and Ed Masterson and Theodore Raymond had come to town with a contract to prepare a five-mile railroad grade between Fort Dodge and Buffalo City. That job done, they'd turned to buffalo hunting.

In preparation for the buffalo hunt, Henry Raymond bought boots for $6.50, a 50-cent pistol scabbard, and a $5 "soldier overcoat." In a small pocket diary purchased at Sedgwick he kept a record of his next year's activities.

Tom Nixon's ranch was located a quarter mile west of town. At Nixon's, Henry found his brother was hunting. Mrs. Nixon encouraged him to stay at the ranch, warning that town was not all that safe.

Theodore showed up on Monday, November 18, and they ate at a restaurant in Dodge, then spent the evening at a dance hall. The brothers did odd jobs over the next couple of days, repairing a wagon, hauling corn and oats and finally, on Thursday, joining the Mastersons who were hunting buffalo at their Kiowa Creek camp, about thirty miles southeast of Dodge City.

Bat Masterson killed four buffalo Henry's first day in camp and the next day Henry helped skin seventeen. Theodore killed five of those. Then on Sunday, November 24, Henry killed two buffalo, as far as is known, his first.

Henry continued as a skinner. They skinned fifteen on Monday and twenty on Tuesday. He'd killed four of those.

Henry recorded seeing packs of wolves, a jack rabbit, and a village of prairie dogs. Ed Masterson shot a wild turkey that first week. By Saturday evening, November 30, they'd killed and butchered eighty buffalo.

On Sunday, December 1, they worked, butchering the buffalo bulls. The numbers for the first week of December, 1872, were: 23, 17, 20, 19, 12 and 26. Abe Mahew and his son Steve from Sedgwick County were working with them and Abe had hauled hides to Dodge and returned December 3, bringing the boys a gallon of whiskey. The next day, a Wednesday, three friendly Arapaho visited. They were the first Indians Henry had seen.

On Sunday, Henry and Ed and Jim Masterson repaid the visit, traveling to the Arapaho camp. Henry noted: "Saw the squaws tanning robes."

It snowed that week and Henry killed his first grouse, saw two Indians picking lice from another's head—and eating them—and he shot "a kyote on run."

Cold weather kept them from working a couple of days and on Sunday, December 15, Henry visited a hunting camp called Big John's and bought a "Navy pistol" for five dollars.

Blowing snow hampered the hunt all week and a bull train must have gotten caught nearby since four bullwhackers spent time with them. Henry, who'd bought a violin when he passed through St. Louis just over a month earlier, played it for them.

Christmas Day began well. Henry wrote that it was a "fine day in morning." They set up a target—a mark—and shot at it. Ed Masterson and Henry were the best shots. About noon, a wind came up and they accepted an invitation to Tom Nixon's camp, located not far away, and Henry played his violin for a stag dance. Another Illinoisan,

Jim White (formerly Jim Wilson) was there that night too. They all stayed the night in a dugout.

Henry and the others returned to their camp the next day and "nearly froze to death." A man, Texan Jim, was in their camp "crazy with tooth ache." Jim and Henry went to "Yahoos to hear boys sing."

They didn't hunt again in December, but prepared their hides, hams and tongues for transport to Dodge City.

On New Year's Day, the weather was bad, but they headed for Dodge anyway. Henry, Abe Mahew and Ed and Jim Masterson all got lost on the prairie in snow and sleet, finally bedding down in the snow. Unable to build a fire, they ate no supper as the sleet and snow continued.

The snow stopped during the night, but they were snowed under. When Henry broke out from under it all, there was a pack of wolves surrounding the little camp. Henry's shots scared them off and before long, the men were rolling toward Dodge. They spent that night at Hunt's Ranch and got to Dodge on Friday. That night they celebrated their safe return by going to the dance hall. Henry wrote that they "heard nice music."

Henry bought a suit of clothes at Collars and went to the dance hall Saturday night. Then on Sunday, Henry sold the buffalo meat they'd butchered at one cent per pound. He used some of his money to eat breakfast and dinner at the hotel. He also bought a can of oysters and a glass of cider. That night, he was back at a dance hall.

The next morning, January 6, Henry bought two sacks of oats, threw them in brother Theodore's wagon and began driving the team home to Sedgwick County, a distance of about 140 miles the way a crow flies. But Henry Raymond chose the normal route, the Santa Fe Trail, which roughly traced the Arkansas River, a distance of about 160 miles.

The route he followed is present U.S. 56. Henry slept outdoors and when he reached Larned, he bought a half-gallon jug of whiskey for $2.50. Rolling past Pawnee Rock, he camped Wednesday night in sight of Great Bend.

The next day, he drove the team past the site of Fort Zarah and on southeast toward Raymond.

Henry spent Friday night in an unfinished sod house. Saturday was a "nice day" and Henry made it five miles or so beyond Hutchinson, camped at "Mr. Dodge's haystack" and ate breakfast with "Mr. Dodge" for ten cents.

Henry got to Sedgwick about 3 p.m., fed the horses, visited the Mahew's and continued on to the Mastersons' in Grant Township.

Henry's brother Theodore was there and over the next days they visited his claim and searched out odd jobs. Henry offered to cut wood for $1.50 per cord. He and Theodore cut posts. They made 105 posts one day, then 41 and 125, and 106 and 94. They hauled the posts with an ox team Theodore had traded for his horses.

On February 18, a Tuesday, Ed Masterson and Henry left for Dodge City. Henry remembered later that the jobs were too scarce in Sedgwick. He wanted to go to Dodge where there was money and work. Ed's dad took them by wagon to Sedgwick and they walked to the train at Newton. Henry bought two pounds of bologna for fifty cents and paid thirty-five cents for crackers. They boarded Car 5167 at 10:20 p.m. "Engine 32, the Kansas," returned them to Dodge City. That night, Henry "heard some splendid music, violin and bass viol and Italian played harp."

Henry spent quite a bit of time in the dance halls and came to know Nell St. Clair and Nell Pool, dance hall girls in Dodge. He learned to play the "Garry Owen," the marching song of the U.S. Seventh Cavalry, "on the accordian by note."

Dodge, suffering the pangs of frontier life, was not always a pleasant place, although exciting for a young man. Two fellows caught a buffalo calf with dogs and tortured it to the point that Henry "shot it to end its misery."

Gunfighter Billy Brooks was shot at from ambush and a soldier was robbed of $5 after being hit over the head with a boot. A buffalo hunter named McGill was shot down by a local vigilance committee. He'd angered locals by shooting a 16-year-old boy on New Year's Day.

During this stay in Dodge, Henry cut wood and unloaded coal from a freight car. Then on March 6, he went buffalo hunting. On this trip southwest of Dodge to the Cimarron River, he saw a "lot of poisoned wolves," antelope, deer, and five wild horses.

By Tuesday, March 18, Henry was back in Dodge and working at Charles Rath & Co., a general merchandise establishment. Henry salted buffalo meat and tongues and baled and loaded buffalo hides on freight cars. For baling hides and loading them and hauling two loads of corn, he received $5. Then Friday afternoon, Henry left Rath's and the next day, joined Tom Nixon's outfit to go hunting.

The hunters saw little game on that Friday, March 21, as they traveled north of Dodge. Nor was there much on Saturday. A storm on Sunday scared their stock off and flipped a spring seat off a wagon onto Henry's head. No serious damage to his head.

Hunting was never good on this trip, so by Friday, Henry was cutting poles again. By Sunday, March 30, he was back at Raths folding buffalo hides and unloading a freight car of oats.

Henry worked for Rath's until April 8, and with the money he made he bought boots ($7.50), a quart of sherry ($1), a shirt ($2.25), a military dress coat ($1.50), and 200 rounds of ammunition ($9). He went hunting again, but was soon back at Rath's.

On April 19, Bat Masterson, Jim White and Henry hired out to kill buffalo for meat for a Dodge City restaurant. They killed eleven, but it wasn't long until Henry took the job of caring for Tom Nixon's and Jim Kelley's race horse, Michigan Jim.

Henry also did other chores around Nixon's ranch, helping plant a garden, making fence, setting out trees, and digging a well.

It was June before Henry went hunting again. The hunters stayed out until June 29 and killed over sixty buffalo, but never more than ten on any one stand. On July 7, Henry went out again, but he stuck a nail in his knee that first night and was laid up. Henry had a rough time with the knee until one of the hunters brought "sugar of lead" to put on the wound nearly a week later.

By Sunday, July 27, the hunters had tallied about 125 buffalo. On that day a violent wind and rain storm scattered their hides a half mile. And then for the next week they saw very little game. Finally, on Wednesday, August 6, Henry, using a gun rest stick he'd cut from hackberry, dropped nine buffalo. By August 12, Henry and the others had loaded forty-five hides (some had been sent earlier) and headed for Dodge. (These sold for 75 cents, plus $1.50 in trade each.)

Henry paid $4 for a hat at Myers and was back chasing buffalo the next day. The killing was slow for about two weeks, then on August 31 Henry dropped a dozen buffalo and his partner Dave Dudley shot three. Things slowed again and they turned back to Dodge on September 6. Their hides brought 80 cents in cash and $1.50 in trade. Henry gave $6 for a pair of boots and forty cents for socks.

On Monday, September 8, Henry "hired to Nixon" to work in Nixon's blacksmith ship. He worked for $30 per month and board. A German named Henry Kramer worked as a blacksmith for Nixon.

Henry Raymond stayed at it until mid-November. During that time, he made hooks, gate hinges, wagon rods, bridle bits, clevises, and lap rings. He fixed gun hammers, neck yokes, axletrees, singletrees, doubletrees, wagon tongues, spring seats, log chains and shovels. He hammered out picket pins, corner straps, bolts, box links, rings, and an iron pump handle. He also shod horses, riveted harness and "put handle in frying pan for cattle man 25 cts."

With his earnings, Henry bought a razor ($2.25); pants, shirt, and vest ($13.50); blanket ($6); pocket knife ($1); clothes ($9) and shoes and socks ($4.20).

On Friday, November 14, Charley Trask gave Henry a Cheyenne ring. Henry gifted Trask with his knife. The next day, after settling up with Tom Nixon, his employer, Henry jumped a freight train headed east. Evidently a railroad man caught him and made him pay $7. He arrived back in Sedgwick County about noon, November 17, 1873.

Henry returned to Dodge City the next winter, but it was getting time to settle down. He married Sarah Armstrong in 1874 and eventually moved to Oklahoma. At Homestead, Oklahoma on October 16, 1936, Henry Raymond died. He's buried at Sunny Dale, back "home" in Sedgwick County, Kansas.

# 11 Rowdy Joe Lowe

Kansas became a stopping-off place, a home away from home, for many during the period immediately following the War Between the States. The cowtowns, a product of the imagination of Joseph G. McCoy, were wild and wide open frontier villages. Lawlessness was rampant, but the cowtowns were places to make money quickly. Some, like Wild Bill Hickok, hired on as lawmen to pursue their fortune. Others, like McCoy, built towns, then owned the hotel or became involved in politics. Still others did as Joe Lowe, born about 1845 or 1846 somewhere in Illinois (some claim Florida). Lowe sometimes operated outside the law. Lowe and his first of seven wives, Kate, also Illinois-born, left their mark on Kansas. And strangely enough, it was a clash with another Illinoisan, Edward T. "Red" Beard, that finally caused the Lowes to move on, leaving Kansas behind.

Perhaps no western towns were ever rowdier than the Kansas cowtowns, nor were many Westerners as rowdy as Rowdy Joe Lowe. He stood 5 feet 9 inches tall, was thick-built with square shoulders, and had a full face. Dark complexioned, he had black hair and wore a heavy black mustache.

Some say Lowe was in Missouri when the Civil War broke out. He enlisted in the Second Missouri Light Artillery and survived the war. After 1865, Lowe worked for a time as a civilian scout for the army. That didn't last long and soon he became interested in operating Kansas dance halls. In that capacity, he was soon recognized as being a menacing character noted for his gruff manners. He was a man to be avoided, unless one sought trouble.

Accompanying Rowdy Joe during many of his years was a slender-built little woman five years younger than Joe. Her maiden name is unknown, but Kansas cowtowns knew her as Rowdy Kate Lowe. Rowdy Kate had light brown hair and was born during 1850 or 1851.

Rowdy Joe was in his early twenties when he arrived in Kansas. He was not notorious yet, but he was working on it. The Junction City (Kansas) *Weekly Union* announced on July 24, 1869: "A man was found drugged and robbed in Ellsworth by fellows known as Jim Bush and Rowdy Joe, the people got after them and in a few days secured the robbers and about seven hundred and fifty dollars of the money. The parties were permitted to leave the country."

Carefully noting the type of justice dealt by Kansans, Rowdy Joe apparently did not stay away long. As a matter of fact, he opened an establishment of note in Ellsworth. When the census taker came around during July 1870, Rowdy Joe and Kate were listed as operators of a "house of ill fame." The embarrassed census taker verified that the Lowes were from Illinois. Joe claimed he was twenty-four; Kate reported that she was nineteen.

That fall Rowdy Joe gained more notoriety. Still in Ellsworth, Joe was accused of stealing "One Slate Colored Mule of the Value of One Hundred and Seventy Five Dollars." For some reason, however, the charges against Joe were dropped. The fate of the mule is unknown.

Nevertheless, Joe's fame and reputation were making it harder form him to make a living. And besides, a new town, Newton, was growing out of the Kansas plains about 65 miles south of Abilene. Railroad work crews of the Atchison, Topeka, and Santa Fe were collecting there. Rowdy Joe and Rowdy Kate suddenly saw fit to move their merchandise to the consuming public, plying their old business, setting up shop in what soon came to be called "Hide Park."

Still in a struggle to become law-abiding, Lowe was indicted during his first summer in Newton by a grand jury for operating a house of prostitution. Kansas courts continued to encourage Rowdy Joe and although no record exists of the outcome of the trial, he continued with business as usual during the remainder of 1871.

Then in February 1872, on an irreverent Sunday evening at Rowdy Joe's place, there was trouble. Several patrons sat around a hot stove trying to drown the loneliness and cold of the Kansas plains with bad whiskey. One of them, a stranger, made some sort of suggestion to

Kate. Astonished at the idea, Rowdy Kate resented the suggestion and said so, offering up an insult of her own to the paying customer.

The February 21, 1872, Topeka *Kansas Daily Commonwealth* reported the results. "The stranger complained to Joe of his treatment, and Joe slapped Kate for the alleged insult. Seizing the opportune moment, a man by the name of A.M. Sweet, formerly of Topeka, 'made up' to Kate, got her drunk and took her to the house of Fanny Grey, formerly of Leavenworth."

Sometime on Monday, Mr. Sweet made a threat on Rowdy Joe's life. A friend of Lowe's, undoubtedly waiting to be of help, rushed right out and found Joe and let him know what Sweet thought of him. Joe, seldom one to let his enemies calm down, marched off to Miss Fanny Grey's "house" and found Sweet. Sweet pulled a revolver, but Rowdy Joe shot him twice before he could use it. Three hours later Sweet gave up the ghost and Lowe gave up to the sheriff. Again Kansas law proved it meant Joe no harm. He was set free.

A few months later Rowdy Joe and Kate were gone south, this time just 26 miles to Wichita — or rather, they went to West Wichita, sometimes called Delano.

Wichita began as a trading post in 1864. It started growing when the railroad extended a branch line down from Newton during May 1872. Signs were soon erected along all incoming roads. Wichitans were eager to capture the cow business and the cowboy's money. The signs proclaimed: *Everything Goes In Wichita.* It was the kind of business climate in which Joe and Kate Lowe could make a fortune and they decided West Wichita was the place for them.

Shortly, their business was open. Their establishment was a dance hall, not a "house of ill repute" — at least not in Kate's and Joe's eyes. Their hall was a place where a lonesome cowhand could, for about 50 cents, have the privilege of bulldozing one of those young lovelies over the sawdust-covered floor in whatever was the dance of the day. Wichita was out on the rough edges of the frontier where men outnumbered women. These dance hall girls mixed with the lonely customers and sometimes made their living by singing, dancing and taking a share from the sale of drinks while they worked. There was music, gaiety, liquor and good times. It was a regular oasis in the middle of a desert, as far as Kate and Joe were concerned. Why, their establishment provided a humanitarian service to south Kansas!

Actually, their business enterprise was of a somewhat depraved nature. Demoted shady ladies from some similar Eastern establishments worked for Rowdy Joe in what was more or less a saloon with the floor space cleared of chairs and tables. There was a music stand, seldom a piano, and normally a few fiddlers and perhaps a pucker-lipped trumpet player to serenade the love-starved lads and their soiled doves. These calico queens were generally imports and often lacking in any of the silk-and-satin qualities portrayed by modern Hollywood standards. They were a gruesome lot with names like Squirrel Tooth Alice, Hambone Jane, Big Nose Kate, Peg-leg Annie—just to name a few of the more outstanding ones.

Regardless, Kate and Joe did well in lawless West Wichita. The Arkansas River marked the boundary of the city limits of Wichita. A bridge at the end of Douglas Avenue was the path followed by those wanting to escape law and order for a few hours of entertainment. It was a roaring good time a curious customer could have "over the river." That is, if he didn't arouse Rowdy Joe's anger.

Since there was no law in West Wichita, it was up to Joe to maintain his own order. And with a pistol in hand he cured most of the ills that beset his establishment. The Wichita *Eagle* (July 26, 1872) reported one such corrective session: "A man by the name of Joseph Walters, who was at the time drunk, was badly bruised and cut about the face and head, by a revolver in the hands of the keeper (Joe Lowe) of the house. Dr. Hendrickson dressed the man's wounds. From what we can learn Walters invited the attack by very disorderly conduct. At this writing the wounded man lies in a very critical condition."

But Joe had his following too. Among those who elevated him to a higher status was a newspaperman out on a raid for the Topeka *Daily Kansas Commonwealth*. He began: "A description of Wichita would be incomplete without a notice of the notorious dance house on the west side of the river, kept by . . . Rowdy Joe, Joseph Lowe, his real name."

The reckless reporter then called on Joe to fill him in so that he could get his story right. His story continued, "Joe has been a frontiersman for many years, and has experienced about as much roughness as any other man. The receipts over his bar average one hundred dollars per night. The receipts are for drinks. No tax is levied for dancing, but it is expected that the males will purchase drinks for themselves and female partners at the conclusion of each dance."

The reporter noted that "Joe is his own

*Rowdy Joe Lowe.*

policeman, and maintains the best of order. No one is disposed to pick a quarrel with him, or infringe upon the rules of his house. A dancing party at this place is unique, as well as interesting. The Texan with mammoth spurs on his boots, which are all exposed, and a broad brimmed sombrero on his head, is seen dancing by the side of a well-dressed, gentlemanly-appearing stranger from some eastern city; both having painted and jeweled courtezans for partners. In the corner of the hall are seen gamblers playing at their favorite games of poker."

Recovering his senses, the reported concluded, "I would not recommend the establishment as one adapted for the schooling of the rising generation, but to those of mature years, who should become acquainted with all phases of society, Rowdy Joe's is a good place to get familiarized with one peculiar phase. While I would not recommend Rowdy Joe as a model for Sunday school scholars, yet I am constrained to say that here are many men passing in society as gentlemen whose hearts are black in comparison with his."

The Topeka reporter left town. Two weeks later Rowdy Joe proved the reliability of his reporting.

Joe and a neighbor had a disagreement. The neighbor was fellow Illinoisan Edward T. Beard. Most called him Red. Red Beard was born some forty-five years earlier. He was the son of the man for whom the town of Beardstown, Illinois on the Illinois River was named. His father was a wealthy man and Red was well educated with "Christian training." Red married a girl from near Virginia, Illinois. According to some reports, they had "three children, two daughters and a son, nearly grown . . . attending school somewhere in the east."

Red Beard abandoned Illinois near the time the Civil War began and roamed over California, Oregon and Arizona, finally returning to Kansas sometime before the incident of October 27, 1873. He was still in search of his fortune.

Normally a jolly, rollicking fellow, according to one who knew him, Beard became upset with Rowdy Joe over some unknown matter the night of Monday, October 27. Ramrod straight despite the amount of liquor he had consumed, Beard, his red curls flowing over his shoulders, burst into his own "dance hall" about 6 p.m.

Jim Goodwin, a one-legged man, came thumping through the door behind him and the two of them approached the bar where Red's bartender Walter Beebe served all sorts of mind-clouding beverages. Red slapped the bar demanding a drink, threw down a glass of whiskey and wiped the enormous mustache under his large nose on the sleeve of his coat.

Staring at Beebe with drunken, glazed eyes, he muttered, "I'm gonna have blood tonight!"

With that, Red turned and walked the length of the dance hall toward his room at the back. Returning in minutes, Red was armed with a big pistol and a shotgun. He said nothing, but sauntered out the door, leaving his place of business, walking off into the night, probably on his way next door to Lowe's place.

What transpired with Red over the next one to two hours has not been determined, except to say he got drunker. And near 8 p.m. he was back in his own establishment, a pistol dangling from his freckled fist. At the end of the room stood a door leading into a hallway. The door had a white knob and Red, without hesitation, raised the big pistol and with two unusually steady hands shot at the knob.

One of Red's customers in the saloon decided he could do better and was anxious to join the fun. He drew his pistol to imitate the owner's shot. But the customer's plans were thwarted. Red took offense and placed his pistol at the patron's head, coldly informing him that if he dared join the fun by shooting the knob, then Red would shoot him. It was a sobering experience for the fun-loving customer.

Nervous smiles soon replaced the long faces in the house as music started several dancing, ending the tense, awkward moment. Beard joined the dancing, forgetting for the moment his earlier threat about having "blood tonight!"

From time to time, Beard walked outside, but he returned each time and seemed to be settling down somewhat. Billie Anderson and Simon K. Ohmert were at the bar and Walter Beebe encouraged them to keep an eye on his boss. Beebe said later, he "was afraid he (Beard) was so drunk that he would get into some trouble."

Just east of Beard's dance hall stood the clapboard building where Rowdy Joe Lowe and Kate had their establishment. There was only fifty feet of space between the two buildings as they faced out onto the street. If interested, a customer in Red's dance hall could look out an east window and peer into Rowdy Joe's place. And that is where Beebe noticed Red standing, by the east window, staring through the black into the dimly lit dance hall owned by Joe Lowe.

Beebe watched his boss slowly raise the pistol again, aim out the window and with both hands, squeeze off a shot. The load shook the hall. Simon Ohmert, former deputy marshal and constable in Wichita, stood nearby. Billie Anderson leaned on the bar and a half dozen or so Texans sat at various places in the room. The girls that worked for Beard were scattered around the room. All were silent, their eyes riveted to the drunken Beard who stood staring out the window, a twisted smile barely pulling at his lips under the red mustache. All waited for the next move. But what would it be?

The front door slammed open! Filling the door, the heavy frame of Rowdy Joe, shotgun held at his hip, stood ready to even the score. Kate was with him and she slipped past Joe into the room, her eyes flashing.

Joe blurted, "Who shot at me?"

From behind the bar, Beebe noticed blood trickling down Lowe's neck and heard Red admit that he was the one that shot Rowdy Joe. But that was all in a moment, because Red's pistol was up and roaring, spitting lead and fire again.

Rowdy Joe's angry shotgun answered the challenge almost in the same instant, the deafening roar drowning the boom of the pistol. Both men missed their mark. Actually Joe's blast came closer to dropping two fleeing Texans, spurs clanging, as the scooted out a side door.

Kate had sized up the situation and decided to abandon her position as well, sliding across the room, also looking for a side exit. Beard was not anxious to face the shotgun and moved toward a door, too, stopping long enough to sling two more shots in Lowe's direction. Someone noticed that Billie Anderson, standing at the bar, had been shot in the head, "the ball passing just back of the eyes." Rowdy Joe raised the shotgun again, but the hammer fell on a bad cap, only snapping at the running Red.

Neither man cared to pursue the fight with the odds so even. Lowe and Beard both fled to the safety of the cold, black night. Before the mumbling patrons could collect themselves and escape, Red appeared, first at a back window, then he was inside demanding that Barkeep Beebe give him his shotgun. Beebe told him, "You left it over in Lowes."

"Oh, no," Red shouted as he reeled toward the back of the hall and his room.

Uneasy moments passed, then after rummaging around looking for the shotgun, Red returned and stood in the hall door, glancing menacingly around the dance hall. At a table was Red's mistress Josephine DeMerritt. "Joe," as she was called, was a local madam who had worked other Kansas towns before coming to West Wichita. Red's watery eyes seemed fixed on her, but there was no romance in them. After a moment, he yelled at her, "Your puttin' up a job on me!"

Fearful and shaking her head as Red walked toward her, Josephine denied it and Red blurted, "Where's my shotgun?"

Josephine said something about him leaving it over in town, referring to Wichita across the bridge. Red, now in a rage, slammed her to the floor, jerked out his pistol and thumbed the hammer, ready to blast her on the spot.

Beebe, Ohmert and a big Texan jumped to Josephine's aid, holding Red until Josephine could pick herself up and flee, stumbling out the front door into the night.

Red calmed some and the men let him up. Beebe asked Red if he was shot. Red said no and shuffled off, finding it hard to keep his feet under him as he moved toward the rear of the room.

At the door, Red just stood there, his eyes heavy-lidded. Then suddenly, without warning, Red raised the murderous pistol and blasted into the hallway. The roar died out as a woman screamed and Red spun and ran across the dance hall and out the front door.

In the hall, Red, under a drunken cloud, had shot Annie Franklin, no doubt thinking he was shooting Josephine DeMerritt.

What caused Red Beard to go on this rampage? The jury is still out on that issue. What is known is that during December, Josephine DeMerritt was convicted of forging a deed to some property owned by Beard. Was Joseph Lowe in cahoots with Josephine DeMerritt? Or was all this a drunken fight?

At any rate, and whatever the cause, later that night Red Beard was blasted by someone with a shotgun. His right arm was shattered at the elbow and he was hit in the hip.

Most figured Rowdy Joe was the culprit, but his defense was that he got so drunk that he was not sure what he did. Indeed, when he surrendered to Michael Meagher, Wichita city marshal, he said as much.

Lowe was standing on the corner at the Progressive Billiard Hall in Wichita when Marshal Meagher walked up. Lowe told him, "I want to give myself up to witnesses."

Meagher said, "I can't take care of you. You'd better go and see Bill Smith (Sheriff of Sedgwick County)."

Together Meagher and Lowe searched out Sheriff Smith, found him and Lowe admitted, "I don't know but what I have shot Red. I just don't know."

Blood still oozed from the wound in Lowe's neck. He explained to Smith and Meagher that "Red shot through the window."

On that information, Rowdy Joe was locked in jail. Red was confined to bed, his wounds not healing. Joe made bail of $2,000 and was let out. And Red grew worse, finally dying on November 11. The Wichita *Eagle* passed judgment, proclaiming, "E.T. Beard, better known as 'Red,' the proprietor of one of the dance houses across the river, paid the penalty of his misdeeds with his life, on Tuesday morning at 3 o'clock a.m."

A few days before Red died, he told his doctor "that he followed the disreputable business only in hopes of getting a start in the world again, but if he got over his wounds he would never go inside a dance house again." Either way, he never went in another one.

West Wichita had settled down by Wednesday, December 10, 1873, when Joe's trial began. The next morning, he was found not guilty, but charges of wounding Billie Anderson and causing other damages were brought against him.

Jail did not appeal to Rowdy Joe and on Saturday, he left it behind him. Sheriff Smith led the posse that pursued the jailbreaker, but the posse came up empty. Smith put out a $100 reward for Lowe's arrest.

In Wichita, on further investigation, Walter Beebe, Rowdy Kate and several others were arrested for helping Joe escape. Others involved in the shooting in October began to run at odds with the law. Simon Ohmert went to jail for perjury. Josephine DeMerritt got ten years in prison for the forgery mentioned above. Rowdy Kate was released from jail and left town "for parts unknown." And Walter Beebe, Beard's friend and bartender, was sentenced to three years in prison for helping his boss' enemy break jail.

But where was Rowdy Joe? When he escaped, every one thought he was GTT—Gone to Texas. But Joe mounted a bay horse and rode due east instead of south, ending the week at Osage Mission (present St. Paul, Kansas), about 110 miles east of Wichita.

The newspaper in Osage Mission proclaimed, "Rowdy Joe the famous Wichitan is in town, and not much rowdy about him after all." But things heated up and on December 18 he fled Osage Mission.

Again law authorities thought he was GTT; again he fooled them. Late in December, Rowdy Kate showed up in Kansas City. She wore a waterproof suit lined in red and had with her two dogs, one a large bulldog, the other a small yellow lap dog. She boarded the Missouri Pacific at 3 p.m. on January 2, 1874, headed for St. Louis.

The next day, before Kate arrived at the Laclede Hotel, detective "Duck" Duckworth arrested A.A. Becker, the alias being used by Rowdy Joe. He was carrying $8,295. St. Louis police had been tipped off by Kansas City officials that Lowe was wanted for jailbreak.

On January 5, Joe was released from jail on a "writ of habeas corpus." Kate had asked for and received his money shortly before this. To some, Joe's unusual release meant that there was a payoff to St. Louis officials. Regardless, Lowe walked quickly from the courtroom, surrounded by friends and wife Kate. A carriage awaited the group and they loaded up and drove swiftly away, apparently leaving St. Louis behind them forever.

Rowdy Joe Lowe's and Kate's lives are at best sketchy from this point in time. In October 1874, Joe was in Denison, Texas making his living from cotton farmers, gamblers and loafers in the little frontier town. By the 29th of the month, the Wichita *Eagle* reported him some 800 miles north and killed in the Black Hills while searching for gold. Indians attacked and "the notorious Rowdy Joe fell first mortally wounded," said the *Eagle*.

Nevertheless, there were occasional references to Joe and Kate through the winter months and the Wichita *Beacon* claimed Joe and Kate were in San Antonio in its March 31, 1875 edition. The San Antonio *Herald* reported Joe very much alive during May 1875: "Mr. Joe Lowe was found guilty of assaulting Kate Lowe yesterday afternoon and fined $100. A motion for a new trial was overruled, and notice of appeal given. The alleged cause for the offense was inconstancy."

Then, like so many of the characters painted into the scenery of the wild and woolly West, Rowdy Joe and Rowdy Kate Lowe faded into the setting sun. Little is known of their whereabouts over their remaining years, although there are reports of Lowe in Dodge City in the 1880s and Denver in the 1890s. Whether they lived long, productive lives is difficult to say.

While one can only speculate as to Kate's fate, there was a report about Joe that perhaps solves the mystery of his fate. The February 15, 1899, Wichita *Eagle* reported that Joe's life was finally done. Claiming that he was seventy-two years old, the *Eagle* reported that he had insulted the Denver Police Department in the presence of a retired Denver policeman in a Denver bar. The retired policeman, according to the story, pulled a gun and shot Rowdy Joe, thus ending the rowdy life of one of the more infamous Westerners.

# 12    The Day Hickok Died

In 1876 with the opening of the Black Hills to gold mining, thousands of adventurous men went west to seek their fortune. They came from all over the United States. One of these men was a youngster from Tazewell County in Illinois named Jerry Bryan. Bryan kept a diary while he was searching for his fortune and in it is recorded an eventful two-day period in Western History. These days were August 2nd and 3rd, 1876. The place was Deadwood, Dakota Territory. Jerry does not have the entire story recorded, but his observations set the mood for the assassination of James Butler "Wild Bill" Hickok.

*August 2: "early this morning . . . a crowd of 20 armed men escorting a Murderer through Town"*

The sun hit Break Neck Hill overlooking Deadwood Gulch about 5:45 a.m. on the morning of August 2, 1876. As the dew was drawn off the canvas and board roof tops of two hundred or so houses, the day grew warmer. Soon miners started gathering their belongings to go off into the hills in hopes of making a bigger strike than yesterday, or the day before, or the day. . . .

The thirty-nine-year-old man awoke from a fitful sleep to find his partners California Joe (Moses Embree Milner) and Colorado Charlie (Charles H. Utter) already stirring around the tent in preparation for the day. It was already hot. He had thrown off the blankets and now sat up. Colorado Charlie spoke first and suggested that he and the man work a short time and then spend the afternoon in the saloon. He readily agreed. The other partner asked if he would like to join him in a trip to Crook City. He had no interest in that suggestion. He was tired from playing cards most of the night and it was nearing mid-day now.

*"About noon a man was found just a cross the creek Dead cause of Death poor whiskey."*

The sun passed high noon and glared down on the tent as Colorado Charlie and the sandy-haired man returned to prepare for the trip to town. He took his time washing as best he could in the stream, trying to get cool so he could stand his clothes. He laid out the Prince Albert coat, the checkered pants, the embroidered silk vest-- his trademark. The patent-leather topped boots with cowboy heels were wiped clean. Soon he donned the .38 rim-fire Richards-Mason conversion pistols (this, according to White-Eye Jack Anderson). The silver-mounted pistols had the butts forward, the way he liked them. The Prince Albert coat was next and then the broad-brimmed black felt hat. As he started through the tent flaps he picked up the carbine fitted into an old-fashioned Kentucky rifle breech. On the stock was engraved the name, J.B. Hickok.

James Butler Hickok had arrived in Deadwood, Dakota Territory about three weeks earlier. He said at the time, "Boys, I have a hunch that I am in my last camp and will never leave this gulch alive." Last night (August 1st) he had felt the same omen. To Tom Dosier, he said, "Tom, I have a presentiment that my time is up and that I am going to be killed." And earlier in the day, he'd posted a letter to his wife of a few months, Agnes.

> Dead Wood Black Hills Dakota
> August 1st 1876

Agnes Darling,

If such should be we never meet again, while firing my last shot I will gently breathe the name of my wife — Agnes — and with wishes even for my enemies I will make the plunge and try to swim to the other shore.

> J.B. Hickok
> Wild Bill

Now the stream that separated the Whitewood camp from town was behind him. The alkali dust rose from the rocky, rutted street. It was too hot for August in Dakota. The few pine trees standing in the street offered no shade. The gambling houses and saloons lined the street on both sides. There was Shingle's Number Three and the Senate, two favorites of Hickok's. The other places of business provided the several other needs of the miners that used Deadwood as a base.

Leander P. Richardson had met Hickok a few days earlier. His magazine article, published in *Scribner's Magazine* during February 1877, described Hickok: "About six feet two inches in height, and very powerfully built; his face was intelligent, his hair blonde, and falling in long ringlets upon his broad shoulders; his eyes, blue and pleasant, looked one straight in the face when he talked; and his lips, thin and compressed, a straw-colored mustache." Richardson wrote that Hickok's "voice was low and musical."

Today, Wild Bill stepped through the front door of Carl Mann and Jerry Lewis' Number Ten saloon. It was about three o'clock when he nodded to his old friend Harry Young, who was tending bar. A poker game was already under way. Carl Mann looked up to his left as Hickok entered and motioned Wild Bill to sit in. Hickok moved toward the table; Charlie Rich had the wall stool. Could he have that stool? Rich laughed. No one's going to attack you, sit here. The place offered was near the back door of the twenty-foot long saloon. Hickok did not like that. It was not his custom to leave his back that open. Missouri steamboat captain William Rodney Massie, age 46, faced the back door. Hickok shrugged, pulled the stool under him and sat down. Still he was uneasy.

Before the cards hit the table, Wild Bill asked Rich to change with him again. This time, Massie, Mann and Rich all joined in the good-natured ribbing of Hickok. Wild Bill sat back down. He was not happy. He took his rifle from his lap and set it against the wall beside Rich. Colorado Charlie entered after a few hands. Hickok was losing. The open back door was more than his concentration could overcome. Captain Massie was getting his money back from the previous night when Wild Bill had beaten him handily.

*James Butler "Wild Bill" Hickok.*

At four o'clock, Colorado Charlie said he was hungry. He had stood, with Hickok's rifle cradled in his arms, beside Rich. Now he set the rifle back in place and left. Hickok did not notice. He was concentrating now; trying to get back in the game.

George M. Shingle stood at the bar busying himself weighing his gold dust. He heard the front door open, turned and saw a drunk come in. The drunk was a slight man. While his one eye was crossed and his nose looked as it had been smashed, he was not unusual for a town full of hard men.

The man ordered whiskey and looked nervously around the room. He saw Shingle at the bar; then Rich, Mann, and Massie. Counting the bartender and Hickok, the drunk saw seven men in the room (the seventh was probably Jerry Lewis, Mann's partner). When his eyes ran across Hickok, he noticed that his back was to the rear door. Hickok looked toward him, but he only asked that Young, the bartender, bring him fifteen dollars in pocket checks. Massie had taken all the money Hickok had with him.

The drunk moved farther down the bar, closer to Hickok's back, but not behind him. Hickok and Massie started arguing. Hickok was irritated. Now in less than six minutes, Massie had taken the pocket checks.

The drunk started out the back door. He got within three or four feet of it, stopped and turned toward Hickok. Shingle heard the dispute between Massie and Hickok getting louder. Hickok said, "The old duffer--he broke me on the hand!" Shingle looked toward the table. The drunk held a pistol in his right hand in back of Hickok's head.

Carl Mann said later, "The pistol was from one foot to eighteen inches from Bill's head. It was a navy sized revolver."

And witness George M. Shingle later described it as "a Sharps improved revolver 18 inches long with a piece of buckskin sewed around the stock."

The startling boom of the big pistol surrounded a strangled cry from the drunk: "Damn you! Take that!"

### "Wild Bill was Shot through the Head Killed instantly."

The bullet entered the "base of the brain, a little to the right of center, . . . exited through the right cheek between the upper and lower jaw bones, loosening several of the molar teeth in its passage," and sped across the table downward and into the wrist of Massie. Mann sat stone-still. Hickok's head jerked down. Massie felt the numbness in his wrist, but did not know why. Shingle moved toward Hickok to look and Young started in the same direction. The drunk pointed the pistol at Young and Shingle and yelled, "Come on ye sons of bitches!" He jerked the trigger. The old pistol snapped twice. It was ten minutes past four.

There was a scramble for the front door. All got out except Mann who was still anchored to his stool. The drunk backed to the door, suddenly turned and ran out. Rich and the others hit the street yelling, "Wild Bill is shot!"

Moments passed while Mann sat on his stool. Then, he watched while Hickok's tall, lithe body eased to the left and fell to the floor. Mann recalled later, "It kind of knocked Bill's head forward and then he fell gradually back." Mann said, "I saw where a bullet came out of his face before he fell."

The body lay there on its side. The knees were drawn up just as they had slid off the stool. By the left hand lay Hickok's last poker hand — the eight of Clubs, the eight of Spades, the ace of Spades, the ace of Clubs, and a Diamond face card (Some say the jack, others, the queen.).

Colorado Charlie received the word of Hickok's death at the camp at Whitewood. A one-horse express wagon was sent to fetch the body and Colorado Charlie went straight to the Number Ten to make sure his friend was really dead. By this time the assassin had been captured in Jacob Shroudy's butcher shop. A crowd was already gathering to decide whether to lynch the man now or later. Suddenly the crowd's attention was turned to a rider coming into town from the north. Indians were attacking Crook City!

### *"Reports come from Crook City that the Indians have Surrounded the Town"*

Every man who had a horse or could borrow one decided to leave Deadwood and go to Crook City and fight the Indians. Meanwhile, Ellis T. (Doc) Pierce, medical man, barber, and undertaker, along with Colorado Charlie and Charlie Anderson busied themselves at the Whitewood camp preparing Hickok's body for display and burial.

Wild Bill Hickok was never more handsome. The corpse was an easy one to prepare. The hole in Hickok's head had drained most of the blood from his body and it took on a marble-like appearance. The sandy hair and flowing mustache were neatly trimmed. The hair was evenly parted with the ringlets over the shoulders framing the face. The several hundred that viewed the body the next day marveled at the dress suit of black broadcloth and the white linen shirt. A reporter wrote, "The arms were folded over the still breast. Beside him in the coffin lay his trusty rifle."

The coffin was as fine as these miners had seen in Deadwood. While it was of rough pine lumber, it had been covered with black cloth outside. The inside was lined with white cloth.

A hasty coroner's jury convened in the Number Ten saloon after the shooting. The foreman, C.H. Sheldon, issued the result, stating that "J.B. Hickock (sic) came to his death from a wound resulting from a shot fired from a pistol in the hands of Jack McCall."

Meanwhile, the assassin, Jack McCall, was being held captive. He said later that month, "I was arrested, lodged in jail and guarded by twenty-five armed men. Great excitement prevailed and I fully expected to be lynched, but another excitement . . . diverted attention from me and preparations were made for a trial."

*"at Sundown a Greaser come in with an Indian Head Wild Bill and every thing else was thrown in the Shade."*

Between eight and eight thirty, a Mexican (some call him Francisco Moros) who had left town with the others to go to Crook City returned. He had found a dead Indian, tried to scalp him, failed, and cut the head off instead. He came riding into Deadwood swinging the head by its long black hair. "The sight of the yelling Mexican and the bloody head caused great commotion in the city and men ran to prepare for an Indian attack, thinking that a real battle was coming." When it was apparent this was not the case "someone perched upon a pile of lumber along the street, pulled out a pair of balance scales and called for contributions." The Mexican was to be rewarded for such a "worthy deed" and soon, sixty-two dollars in gold dust was given him. The Mexican then left for Crook City. He was shot later that night.

Deadwood soon settled down to a normal night of hell-raising. A mass meeting at McDaniel's theater appointed the officials for tomorrow's trial of McCall and out at the Whitewood camp in the pines north of Deadwood's main street, "White-Eye" Jack Anderson sat patiently with the "Prince of Pistoleers," watching the coffin "to see that nothing bothered it."

*August 3: "the Trial of the assassin . . . come off to day"*

Notices appeared around town early the morning of the third. On black-bordered paper, they read:

Died, in Deadwood, Black Hills August 2, 1876, from the effect of a pistol shot, J.B. Hickok, (Wild Bill) formerly of Cheyenne, Wyoming. Funeral Services will be held at Charlie Utter's camp, on Thursday afternoon, August 3, 1876, at 3 o'clock. All are respectfully invited to attend.

After a short session in the morning, the trial reconvened at two o'clock. Jurors were chosen, witnesses were called, McCall's character witnesses testified, and when McCall took the stand he said, "Wild Bill killed my brother, and I killed him. Wild Bill threatened to kill me if I ever crossed his path. I am not sorry for what I have done. If I had to, I would do the same thing over again."

At three o'clock at Colorado Charlie's camp, friends and a large number of curious onlookers surrounded an open grave. The pallbearers—Bill Hillman, John Oyster, Charlie Rich, Jerry Lewis, Charlie Young, and Tom Dosier—let the pine box down gently and evenly into the grave, someone tried to say the appropriate words, and soon another began to throw dirt on this legendary man. The son of William Alonzo and Polly Butler Hickok of Troy Grove, La Salle County, Illinois had ridden a long and difficult trail to gain this humble end. A simple marker at the head of the grave, either on a board or carved into a stump, said;

A brave man; the victim of an assassin—J.B. (Wild Bill) Hickock, age 48 years; murdered by Jack McCall, August 2, 1876.

In the years that followed, the body was moved to Mount Moriah Cemetery where first a bust of Hickok and later a life-sized sandstone statue came under attack from relic-hunting tourists. The gravesite stands five hundred feet above Deadwood and offers the visitor a spectacular view of the region.

*"Result of the Trial was, Turned him loose to kill some body else"*

*The town where Hickok died—Deadwood, Dakota Territory, during 1876.*

At seven thirty, Charles Whitehead, foreman of the jury, rose and facing the judge, W.S. Kuykendall, said, "We, the jurors, find the prisoner, Mr. John McCall, not guilty."

*"It is getting to dangerous here to be healthy. A man is liable to be shot here any time by Some Drunken Desperado . . . this is our last night in Dead Wood"*

During the next days and months, Jack McCall found it in his best interests to get out of the Black Hills country. A few weeks later, while drunk, McCall boasted about the killing and was arrested by a Deputy U.S. Marshal named Balcombe. McCall was brought to trial in Yankton, Dakota Territory. The new trial was brought about because the Deadwood trial had been illegal. The Black Hills were still a part of Indian Territory due to the 1868 Laramie Treaty with the various tribes. Whites were not even supposed to be in Deadwood or the Black Hills. This new trial was initiated on October 18, 1876, when McCall entered a "Not Guilty" plea. He tried to break jail on November 9 and his trial finally got under way on December 4, 1876, Chief Justice P.C. Shannon presiding. The Yankton, Dakota Territory jury retired at 7 p.m. on December 6 and returned a "Guilty" verdict at 10:15 p.m.

Testimony in this trial revealed facts which contradicted the previous illegal trial. Hickok had not shot the brother of McCall in Kansas. It is doubtful that McCall even had a brother. He does appear to have had three sisters, a father and mother living in Louisville, Kentucky—this based on a letter received by United States Marshal Burdick at Yankton on February 28, 1877. In the letter, the sender, Mary A. McCall, was in search of her brother. She wrote, "This John McCall (sic) is about twenty-five years old, has light hair, inclined to curl, and one eye is crossed." John McCall, alias Jack McCall, fit this description exactly.

McCall spent his last days writing letters, reading the *Bible* and visiting with a Catholic priest. The morning of March 1, 1877, was dreary, cloudy and rainy. McCall was loaded into a wagon, the featured character in Yankton County's first legal hanging, and hauled two miles out of town to "the school section north of the Catholic cemetery." At precisely 10:15 a.m., John McCall's body fell four feet through the trap. With a strangled "Oh, God," James Butler Hickok was avenged.

McCall was buried in a corner of the Catholic cemetery.

# 13

# The Earps

Wyatt Earp was born in Warren County, Illinois at the county seat of Monmouth on Sunday, March 19, 1848. Nicholas and Virginia Ann Earp and their new son resided on the east side of the 200 block of South Third Street. (In September 1955, a large granite monument was dedicated at 406 South Third Street. The house itself is now located at 913 South Sixth.)

Wyatt Berry Stapp Earp, the man, was feared, loved, accused, acquitted, admired and hated. In death, with the publication of a controversial biography, he was finally honored. The movies and television tend to glorify the hero, making it unusually difficult to discover the truth about the man. But then the truth begins for every person at birth and birth is where the story of Wyatt Berry Stapp Earp begins.

But first, Walter Earp. Wyatt's grandfather came to Monmouth via Virginia, Maryland, North Carolina and Kentucky. Wyatt's father, Nicholas Porter Earp, was born in North Carolina. Nicholas' first wife, Abigail Storm, gave him two children, both born at Hartford (Ohio County), Kentucky. But she died and in 1840, Nicholas married Wyatt's mother. Still at Hartford, James C. was born in 1841 and Virgil W. in 1843.

By 1847, Walter Earp was Justice of the Peace in Illinois' Monmouth township. His son and grandchildren settled on a nearby farm. For a time Nicholas owned a small saloon, but the Mexican War took him away. His unit was mustered in at Quincy, Illinois and commanded by a former member of the Illinois House and Senate, Captain Wyatt Berry Stapp. Just months later, Nicholas was back home in time for the birth of the son he would name after his commander.

*Wyatt Earp. (Courtesy of the Arizona Historical Society.)*

Nicholas was discharged after being kicked by a mule at Magdalena, Mexico.

The next year, the Earps grew restless. Like so many of that day, they packed their belongings and rode wagons west. The Earps stopped at Pella, Iowa some forty miles southeast of Des Moines. There, in Pella, the last two Earp brothers were born—Morgan, during 1851 and Baxter Warren in 1855.

Still they were not settled. In 1856, Nicholas Earp and his family returned to Illinois and Monmouth where they lived for two more years. In 1859, they returned to Iowa. Their next stop was Montgomery County, Missouri and by the time the Civil War commenced, the Earps were back at Pella, Iowa. The five-foot, eight-inch James Earp returned to Warren County to join the 17th Illinois Infantry. (The war ended for him less than a year later when he was wounded not far from Cape Girardeau, Missouri. His crippled left shoulder reminded him of that day at Fredericktown, Missouri the rest of his life.) Virgil, too, returned to Monmouth and joined the 83rd Illinois Infantry.

As soon as Jim returned wounded from the war, Nicholas decided to try California. The Earps joined a wagon train in Omaha, Nebraska on Thursday, May 12, 1864, and arrived seven months later in San Bernardino. Still not satisfied, in 1869 the Earps returned east, landing this time in Lamar (Baxter County), Missouri.

On January 10, 1870, Wyatt married Willa Sutherland of Lamar. Before 1870 was done, Willa was dead and Wyatt had his first law enforcement job. He was town constable, but not for long. By mid-1871, he had chased around Kansas hunting buffalo, drifted into Indian Territory (Oklahoma) where he was arrested for horse theft, permitted to post $500 bond, skipped town, and became a federal fugitive. (This occurred near Fort Gibson, Oklahoma).

Wyatt stayed clear of Oklahoma, but continued hunting buffalo until 1874 when Wichita, Kansas became home. Morgan joined him and brother Jim was already tending bar at Charley Shattner's Custom House Saloon and sporting a new wife, Nellie Bartlett Ketchum, a Monmouth widow Jim wed in 1873. Wyatt took a job as policeman for $2 a day, hired from month to month. He was dismissed before serving a year.

In May 1876, Wyatt signed on as a policeman in Dodge City, Kansas. He quit in September and drifted to Deadwood, Dakota Territory where a gold rush attracted miners and other gamblers.

Back in Dodge City by the summer of 1877, Wyatt was rehired and worked until November as a policeman. Nothing much happened, except that Wyatt brawled with one of the local "painted cats," Frankie Bell. Wyatt was arrested and fined a dollar for fighting with the woman.

Texas was Wyatt's next stop. He gambled at Fort Griffin and dealt cards in the Cattle Exchange Saloon at Fort Worth before returning to Dodge City in May 1879. The Dodge City *Times* was pleased: "Wyatt Earp . . . has just returned from Fort Worth, Texas. He was immediately appointed Asst. Marshal, by our City dads, much to their credit."

This time, Wyatt was a busy man. He was deacon of the Union Church, doubled his law enforcement income dealing faro and monte at the Long Branch Saloon, and greeted old friends and made new ones.

One of the old friends was Bat Masterson, the dapper Sheriff of Ford County, Kansas. A newspaper called Masterson: "A cool, brave man, pleasant in his manners, but terrible in a fight." A gambler like Wyatt, Masterson could often be found in the Long Branch, owned by another Earp friend, Luke Short. Short was a quick-tempered character who some say was too willing to kill. A little man, he was noted for crowding his victim then blasting him with a .45. One Westerner claimed Short shot from such close range because "that way, he got the effect of the muzzle blast. It knocked the other man off balance. The .45 burned terribly at close range. It was impossible to face it. . . ." Strangely, Short died peacefully—at age 39.

Another Earp friend announced his entry to Dodge City in the Dodge City *Times,* June 8, 1878:

## DENTISTRY

J.H.Holliday, Dentist, very respectfully offers his professional services to the citizens of Dodge City and surrounding country during the summer. Office at room No. 24, Dodge House. Where satisfaction is not given money will be refunded.

Better known as Doc Holliday, this tall, slender son of Georgia was educated in Baltimore before discovering that he was dying of chronic pulmonary tuberculosis. In search of dry climate, he visited Texas, Denver and finally, Dodge City. With him was Katherine Elder, better known as Big Nose Kate. Holliday claimed sometimes that they were married in St. Louis at the Planter's Hotel. Holliday was ill-tempered, especially when drinking. Since he was an alcoholic, that was most of the time. And he gambled. He too died calmly, and probably drunk, in a Glenwood Springs, Colorado sanatorium during 1887. He was 35.

And Wyatt's brothers remained in touch during this time too. Virgil, five years older than Wyatt, drove a stage, prospected for silver, and after moving to near Prescott, Arizona in 1876, worked as part-time deputy sheriff. The younger Morgan was an occasional policeman and laborer. He joined Wyatt at Dodge.

Jim Earp wasn't much like his brothers. He was shorter and the crippled arm from the Civil War made him the more passive of Nicholas and Virginia's sons. Generally, Jim tended to business as a saloonkeeper, avoiding trouble.

Suddenly, after only four months in Dodge, Wyatt quit his assistant marshal job and headed for Las Vegas, New Mexico. There was talk of starting a stage line, but Wyatt was drawn off that course by a silver strike in the San Pedro Valley of Arizona Territory.

Jim and Wyatt and their wives continued west in wagons to meet with Virgil and his wife at Prescott. Doc Holliday and Kate joined them and together they headed their wagons southeast. By November 27, 1879, they were all in Tucson where Virgil received an appointment as Deputy U.S. Marshal under the U.S. Marshal at Tucson, L.F. Blackburn. (Virgil was the only Earp to hold a regular commission as a U.S. Marshal or deputy.)

Windswept Dodge City lay many miles and several months behind when the Earps and their wives first viewed the dust-blown plateau that lay between the Dragoon and Whetstone Mountains in southeastern Arizona. Less than a mile square that Monday, December 1, 1879 when the Earps arrived, the tent-infested little town of Tombstone would take on some prominence in the next couple of years. The legends would grow about the town almost as fast as the legends grew about these long-legged strangers with their drooping mustaches and dust-covered, wide-brimmed hats and long coats.

Fremont Street was Tombstone's widest and the Earps' wagons tracked slowly along it. The gaming houses that the Earps knew so well were not on Fremont, but one block over on Allen Street. That was where the Earps would spend most of their time. That was where their style of life was fed. That was the street in Tombstone that was quiet, almost deserted, by day. That was the street that came to life as the sun fell away letting miners, cowboys and gamblers slip around under cover of darkness. And it was Allen Street that a nighttime traveler heard miles away in the quiet desert surrounding Tombstone.

*Morgan Earp. (Courtesy of the Arizona Historical Society.)*

One visitor remembered: "The noise was harmless unless it bothered you, and then it drove you crazy."

While Virgil, Wyatt and Jim were on Allen Street "sizin' up the town" their wives sewed clothes and awnings for a penny a yard. It wasn't long until Jim got a job dealing faro. And soon after Wyatt took a job with Wells, Fargo as a shotgun messenger.

Life wasn't easy in Tombstone. Water sold for three cents a gallon. It was hauled in by wagon. The only wood available for heat and cooking was mesquite scavanged from the desert. Rats were a gnawing problem in some areas of town. Still the town grew.

Tombstone was not Wichita, Dodge or Ellsworth where all hell broke loose when the summer cowboys drove their herds north. By 1880, Tombstone had four churches and the way things were going on Allen Street, a need for more. The school system was a good one. This was a mining town. There was money the year around.

During 1880 brother Morgan arrived and replaced Wyatt with Wells, Fargo. Wyatt took an appointment as deputy sheriff of Pima County for a short time. Virgil helped out the local police, waiting for a full-time job.

Then in October, Town Marshal Fred White was gunned down "accidently" by a cowboy sometimes called Curly Bill Brocius. Virgil Earp took over the job until a special election could be held in November 1880.

The November special election left Virgil Earp a loser to Ben Sippy. Still not willing to give up, Virgil ran against Sippy in the regular January 1881 election. He lost again.

Although disappointed, the Earps were glad that their Republican friend, John P. Clum, was elected mayor of Tombstone. Clum had arrived in Arizona eight years earlier. He was the agent on San Carlos Apache Reservation before coming to Tombstone as editor of the *Tombstone Epitaph.*

For some time, Wyatt eyed — and coveted — the upcoming position of county sheriff. Tombstone was in Pima County, but was destined to be re-organized into Cochise County. Now, in January 1881, with a Republican mayor in Tombstone and a Republican Territorial Governor, John C. Fremont, Wyatt figured he had the appointment cinched.

Then Cochise County was formed. Tombstone became the county seat as planned, but a polished Arizona native of 18 years, Democrat John Harris Behan was appointed sheriff! Behan, in his thirties, had served as sheriff of Yavapai County, deputy sheriff of Pima County, and was in business at Tombstone's Dexter Livery Stable.

The sheriff's job meant Behan was the county tax collector. Some estimated that Behan's share of the taxes amounted to thirty or forty thousand dollars a year.

A dejected Wyatt Earp settled into a new job. He owned part of the gambling concession in the Oriental Saloon, a bar one visited carefully. And when business was slow, Wyatt dealt faro at the Eagle Brewery across the street. An old friend from Dodge City, Bat Masterson, showed up soon to deal at the Oriental. Luke Short got there not long after, joining Wyatt, his brothers and Doc Holliday. But the Earps were making new friends in Tombstone too. Among them were Newman Haynes Clanton's sons and the McLowry brothers, Tom and Frank. (McLaury is the contemporary spelling, but in Tombstone, the spelling was McLowery or McLowry. See *Tombstone Epitaph,* October 27, 1881—actually, the name was originally McClaughry.) Together with Luke Short and Doc Holliday; Wyatt and Morgan Earp, Billy and Ike Clanton, and Tom McLowry posed for a photograph during the spring of 1881. Tombstone and the "Earp gang" were a picture of tranquility.

Then on March 15, the Tombstone-to-Benson stagecoach was held up. No money was lost, but two men, Eli "Bud" Philpot and Peter Roerig, were murdered. Rumors chased rumors and all Tombstone was buzzing. Some said Doc Holliday was the killer and Wyatt Earp, with the help of his friend, Wells, Fargo agent Marshall Williams, planned the holdup.

Another story had Wyatt offering money to Ike Clanton for Ike's help in catching three men that helped Doc stop the stage. Earp, according to the story, would kill them, eliminating the witnesses against his friend, Doc.

Did Doc Holliday kill the men on the stage? Doc was out of town that night. Ike Clanton testified later that Wyatt Earp offered him money to help trap the three stage robbers. Some say Billy Clanton saw Doc do it.

Regardless, there was enough doubt to cause the Earps and Holliday to suffer some loss of reputation. Even their friends, Luke Short and Bat Masterson decided they should be someplace else following the stage killings. Through April and May matters did not improve, but then in June there was a turn for the better. On June 6, Town Marshal Ben Sippy left town and Virgil took over the job permanently. And if there were still rumors about the Earps, they faded some the evening of June 22 when a bad barrel of whiskey exploded, setting fire to a saloon and causing sixty-six businesses to go up in smoke. Rumors about the Earps were replaced with talk about the big fire. The same day, two of the fugitives in the March stage murders were killed attempting a holdup in New Mexico. Indeed, the Earps seemed on their way back.

*Virgil Earp.*
*(Courtesy of the*
*Arizona Historical*
*Society.)*

Then on July 5, Kate Elder, who for one reason or the other was irritated with Doc Holliday, stomped into the sheriff's office and on the strength of an affidavit, Behan swore out a warrant for Doc for the stage-holdup murders. Holliday was arrested, but within three or four days the case was dismissed for lack of evidence. Immediately, Doc swore out a warrant for Kate, saying she had threatened his life. The charges were dropped after Kate was arrested and decided to move on to Globe, Arizona within the week. (Kate opened a boarding house in Globe. Some say she remarried and died in a "pioneer's home.")

Rumors continued to fly through the hot, dusty streets of the mining metropolis. Some were saying the Clantons and McLowrys thought Tombstone would be a better place with the Earps gone. In August, "Old Man" (he was about 65) Clanton was ambushed, some said by Mexican soldiers out to stop the rustling of Mexican cattle.

This ambush, according to the Tucson *Arizona Weekly Star* (August 25, 1881), took place in Guadalupe Canyon, New Mexico. Besides Clanton, several other Americans were killed. Someone figured they were attacked by 20 or 30 Mexicans. This story has Clanton's gang ambushing Mexican smugglers in the Peloncillo Mountains early in August and hauling off $4,000 in loot. The Mexicans, possibly soldiers from Fronteras, killed Clanton and the others on August 13 for revenge. A grizzled, bearded, rough-looking man, Newman H. Clanton and his neighbors, the McLowrys, are generally acknowledged to have been rustling cattle on occasion—and if not rustling, then certainly harboring rustlers on their ranches. However, Cochise County Deputy Sheriff Bill Breakenridge pointed out in later years, "If there was ever a warrant for the McLowerys or Clantons, I never heard about it—and I would have heard about it, for my particular job was the serving of warrants for men outside of Tombstone." The *Tombstone Epitaph* of August 19, 1881 already contained an argument for the sheriff: "There is altogether too much good feeling between the sheriff's office and the outlaws infesting this country."

The stage robberies continued through the summer. In September there was a robbery for which T.C. "Frank" Stilwell (a former Behan deputy) and Pete Spence (an Earp friend) were arrested by posses led by Behan and Deputy U.S. Marshal Virgil Earp. Stilwell and Spence were co-owners of the Bisbee Livery Stable. Returned to Tombstone, the two were released on bail made by Ike Clanton. Frank McLowry, on hearing of the situation, some say, told Morgan Earp, "If you ever come after me, you'll never take me."

By October, the stage was set. Toward the end of the month conditions would be such that in less than a minute thirty to fifty rounds of ammunition would explode leaving three dead and three wounded—and somehow making Wyatt Earp a legend. The killings were not in, but near the O.K. Corral; the killing took place between Camillus Fly's part-time rooming house and Photograph Gallery and William Harwood's privately-owned little frame house.

Why did the killings take place? It is doubtful that anyone will ever be able to answer that for the legend has blotted and smeared the truth for over a century. Some have speculated (guessed?) that the

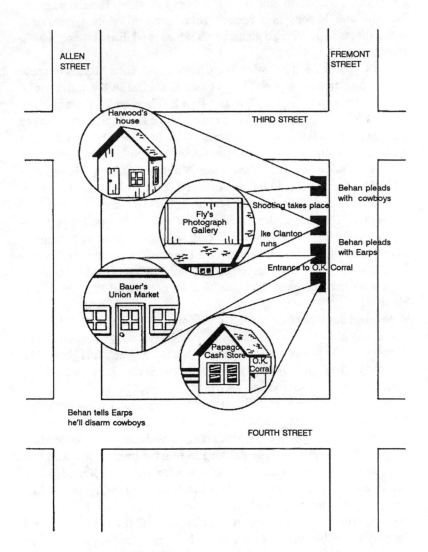

**Tombstone — October 26, 1881**

Earps feared the Clantons would tell all. Others have the Earps trying to get the Clantons to hold a stage robbery in which the Earps might become the heroes and restore their credibility in Tombstone. Regardless, word spread that the Clantons and Earps were having trouble.

On October 25, a Tuesday, Ike Clanton and Tom McLowry came into Tombstone by wagon. They'd eaten breakfast at Chandler's milk ranch with their brothers Billy and Frank. Then while Ike and Tom headed for town, Billy and Frank rode toward the McLowry ranch to round up stock. Ike and Tom expected their brothers the next day. Ike came to visit the saloons and gamble. After drinking and gambling until after midnight, Ike entered the Alhambra Saloon. He sat at a table near the lunch counter, and ordered something to eat. Doc Holliday arrived and walked to Ike's table. In his usual unpleasant mood, Doc cursed Ike and challenged him to get a gun. Morgan Earp, working as a policeman, was urged by Wyatt, who was at the lunch counter, to break up the argument. Morgan led Doc out the back door; Ike followed. While the bickering continued, Ike walked off into the night. He found another game and gambled away most of the rest of the night.

Wednesday, October 26, 1881: The sun slipped into the Arizona sky shortly after six a.m. that fateful October morning. Allen Street lay sleeping but that was not strange. It slept until noon most days. The bartender from the Oriental Saloon shook Wyatt Earp awake just before noon. Ike Clanton was on the prowl—and he was armed.

Shortly, Virgil deputized Wyatt and Morgan and they went prowling after Ike Clanton. Within minutes Virgil found the bleary-eyed cowboy, stripped him of the rifle he carried and with Morgan, led him to court. The bewildered Ike paid a $25 fine for toting a gun and was turned loose. Tall, slender Billy Claibourne, a friend of Ike's, led him to a doctor named Gillingham. Ike's head needed tending; Virgil had layed it open with his pistol barrel.

Tom McLowry had stayed at a different hotel than Ike, but heard Ike was in trouble and went searching for him. Some say the solemn-faced Tom ran into Wyatt after Ike's court hearing and others claim Wyatt and Tom met up the street. All agree that Wyatt, for no apparent reason, shoved and then pistol-whipped Tom McLowry, leaving him bleeding in the dusty street.

In the meantime, Frank McLowry and Billy Clanton rode into Tombstone. They had errands and went about doing them. Billy Claibourne found them and explained their brothers' troubles. Ike, his head wrapped in gauze, came along and before he could speak, Billy Clanton berated him and insisted that he get home. Billy told Claibourne, "I don't want to fight anybody and nobody wants to fight me." They all walked toward the O.K. Corral.

Two hours had slipped by since Oriental bartender Ned Boyle stirred Wyatt awake. The Earps—Wyatt, Virgil and Morgan—now stood in front of Hafford's Saloon. Doc Holliday, his pasty-white face grayer than usual, sauntered up wearing a gray coat. His only visible weapon was a cane clinched in his fist.

Somehow the Earps looked taller and more villainous this quiet Tombstone afternoon. Their sagging black mustaches matched the black Stetsons and greatcoats that became a part of their legend. All carried revolvers and Virgil packed a shotgun—probably a 12-gauge. As one, the group moved to the corner of Allen Street and Fourth.

Sitting in a nearby barbershop, his long frame laid back and a barber's cold razor scraping away the whiskers, was Sheriff John Behan. The barber was busy bringing Behan up to date on the morning's events. Casually, the barber mentioned that the Earps were out there with a crowd gathering around them right now.

Behan got out of the chair and, grabbing his hat, made his way to the corner and told Virgil Earp he'd take the cowboy's guns if they'd just give him time. Behan then turned and strode down Fourth Street to Fremont to find the McLowrys and Clantons.

Several minutes slipped by; the Earps waited impatiently. The crowd grew impatient with them. Someone suggested the cowboys were just over on Fremont. Using that as a cue, the Earps headed for Fremont Street. Holliday walked with him, trading his cane to Virgil for the shotgun.

On Fremont, they stared past the Papago Cash Store and O.K. Corral sign, spotting Behan talking with the cowboys. None stopped; their strides remained the same, pulling them closer to where Behan pleaded with the Clantons and McLowrys. The Earps and Holliday passed the corral entrance and walked under the awning of Bauer's Union Market. Behan stood there now, ready to plead his case with the Earps. He begged, but the Earps pushed by him, determined now to finish the job.

Just past Fly's Photograph Gallery, the Clantons and McLowrys waited, their eyes riveted on the fast-closing Earp bunch, Behan cringed and moved out of the line of fire, slipping in beside Fly's. The Earps stopped suddenly between the Gallery and Harwood's house. The tiny lot was only twenty feet wide and Billy and Ike Clanton were in it, their backs to the house. Virgil Earp paced to within six feet of them, Doc's cane at his side. At the edge of the street Wyatt and Doc glared at Tom and Frank McLowry. Morgan was just to Doc's right and Frank McLowry's horse was between Frank and Tom. Six feet separated the opponents when guns exploded, shattering the two o'clock quiet of the town called Tombstone.

Just a couple short blocks away, Virgil Earp's wife remembered, "The noise was awful . . . I jumped up and ran out the door. I knew it had come at last. People all over were runnin' toward the O.K. Corral."

When Virgil's wife Allie arrived, breathless, she sought only her man, her "Virge." The shotgun blast that killed and hurled Tom McLowry away, left him sprawled alone at the corner of Third and Fremont. Allie raced by him. She only glanced at the mortally wounded Billy Clanton as grim-faced men carried the nineteen-year-old across the street. Then after she asked, someone took her to Virgil. He was shot in the calf, but conscious.

The others? Frank McLowry was dying, as had been Billy Clanton. Morgan was hit in the shoulder and Doc's hip took a bullet. Ike Clanton was safe somewhere. He ran when the shooting started. And Billy Claibourne managed to slip inside Fly's Gallery with Sheriff Behan.

And what exactly took place at "the shoot-out at the lot between Fly's and Harwood's?" Who knows?

One witness swore, "The Earps called out, 'Hands up' and began firing almost simultaneously." Another insisted, "Tom McLowery had his hands up when a load of buckshot cut him down." A mining engineer saw the fight and said, "To be plain it was simply cold-blooded murder."

During the hearing before Magistrate Wells Spicer, an attorney friend of the Earps, a half dozen witnesses testified that the Clanton-McLowry group surrendered before being gunned down. Others claimed that Billy Clanton and Frank McLowry (the only ones armed—both packed Colt Frontier 1873 single-action revolvers) returned the fire after they were fatally wounded. Other depositions by witnesses claimed Virgil commanded, "Throw up your hands!"

Some thought Wyatt called out, "You sons of bitches have been looking for a fight and now you can have one!"

Billy Clanton, his hands up, shouted, "Don't shoot me! I don't want to fight!"

And the shooting started. The *Tombstone Nugget* claimed there were 30 shots fired in 25 seconds.

On October 29, Virgil was suspended from his position as town marshal and Billy, Tom and Frank went on display in a hardware store window. A sign above them read: *Murdered In The Streets Of Tombstone.*

That night George Whitwell Parsons, a Tombstone resident, sat down and recorded the events of Wednesday in his diary: "A bad time yesterday when Wyatt, Virgil, and Morgan Earp with Doc Holliday had a street fight with the two McLowrey's and Bill Clanton and Ike, all but the latter being killed and V. and M. Earp wounded. Desperate men and a desperate encounter. Bad blood brewing for some time and I am not surprised at the outbreak. It is only a wonder it has not happened before. . . ."

As a result of the inquest, Wyatt and Doc were jailed for murder. (Morgan and Virgil were still bedfast from wounds.) Wells Spicer's hearing lasted until December 1. His ruling: "There being no sufficient cause to believe the within named Wyatt S. Earp and John H. Holliday guilty of the offense mentioned within, I order them to be released."

Spicer's verdict was not popular. But local newspapers were split over the matter. While the *Tombstone Nugget* claimed the Clantons and McLowrys were "harmless cowboys mercilessly hounded by the ruffian Earps," the *Epitaph* said the Earps were "honest defenders of justice" and that the Clantons and McLowrys were "ruthless outlaws bent on destroying the town."

Within two weeks, someone tried to murder Mayor John Clum; Wells Spicer was warned against staying in Tombstone; and a citizen's committee reportedly warned the Earps that any further action such as that of October 26 would result in their hanging—no hearing, no trial; just rope, noose and hanging tree.

But it wasn't just warnings. On December 28, Virgil Earp was shot from ambush. Buckshot tore into his side, back and elbow, but he lived. Until March 18, Virgil's wife nursed him back to health in a room at the two-year-old Cosmopolitan Hotel. On that night fate—an assassin—struck the Earps again. Morgan and Wyatt were shooting pool in Campbell and Hatch's Saloon and Billiard Hall on Allen Street. Two shots split the stale, beer smell of the pool room. One bullet tore Morgan's spinal column in two. He died where he fell a half hour later. The bullet for Wyatt was inches too high, plowing into the wall above his head.

Two days later, the Earps and several friends escorted Morgan's corpse out of Tombstone, headed for Colton, California, their parent's home. That night at Tucson as the train pulled out of the station headed west, shots rang out; the next morning, Ike Clanton's friend, Frank Stilwell was found with two shotgun blasts and four rifle slugs in his dead body. (Later, on two occasions, Wyatt claimed he killed Stilwell to avenge his dead brother. Wyatt said he used a pistol. Most figure Holliday was there too.)

Wyatt returned to Tombstone, deciding against the California trip in favor of the search for others involved in his brother's murder. Sheriff Behan was ready to arrest him for Stilwell's murder, but decided against it. On March 21, Wyatt rode out of Tombstone for the last time.

With the murder warrant chasing him, Wyatt fled Arizona and showed up near Gunnison, Colorado not long after. The Arizona Territorial Governor asked for Wyatt's extradition, but was refused. Finally the charges were dropped. Having abandoned his mate, Mattie Blaylock Earp, Wyatt found another in San Francisco. He and

Josephine Sarah Marcus stayed together through the years that Wyatt roamed Colorado, Kansas, Wyoming, Idaho and Texas. They were seen in San Diego where Wyatt owned a saloon. They attended the Chicago World's Fair in 1893 and went to Alaska together in 1897. Tonopah, Nevada attracted saloonkeeper Earp in 1902 and finally, during 1906, he and Josephine settled down in Los Angeles.

On January 13, 1929, Wyatt Earp died at 4004 West 17th Street in Los Angeles. Two of those at the funeral were former Tombstone Mayor John Clum and the man with the diary, George W. Parsons.

Wyatt's father, Nicholas Porter Earp, had died in 1907 at the Soldier's Home at Sawtelle, near Los Angeles. Brother Jim died in 1926 and Virgil lost to pneumonia in 1906. As for the baby, Warren, who wanted so much to be like his older brothers, he was shot to death sometime not long after 1900.

# 14    Allan Pinkerton and the West

In 1871 a terrible fire brought Chicago to its knees. In 27 hours, 17,450 buildings turned to ashes and smoke. Included in the ashes was the Pinkerton's National Detective Agency.

The office was rebuilt and four years later in 1875, a young, oval-faced outlaw from Missouri stood staring across a busy street at the entrance. The outlaw sought the man who ran the agency, Allan Pinkerton. He wanted to kill Pinkerton to even a score. The young man's name: Jesse James.

Pinkerton agents were blamed for an attack on the home of Jesse's mother, killing Jesse's half-brother and seriously injuring Jesse's mother. Now just weeks later, according to Jesse's Uncle George Hite, Jesse was in Chicago stalking Allan Pinkerton. But the time was never right and Pinkerton lived. Jesse claimed later that to kill Pinkerton "was too easy. When I do it, I want him to know it's me who's doing it."

By this time Allan Pinkerton had been fighting crime for a quarter of a century. He lived at a time when crime flourished throughout the United States. In the East, the Methodist bishop of New York assessed his city, counted Methodists, then gangsters and prostitutes, and concluded that the Methodists were outnumbered.

That was in 1866 and Allan Pinkerton was in Illinois after working for the government as undercover agent Major E.J. Allen and establishing a Union Army secret service.

With offices in Chicago and several other cities, Pinkerton and his detectives waged war on outlaws not only in the East, but in the wild and woolly West.

Some date the Pinkerton pursuit of the James Gang from the Ocobock Brothers Bank in Corydon, Iowa. The bank lost $6,000 (some say $45,000) on June 3, 1871. The brazen James brothers not only robbed the bank but rode to the local church, interrupted a political speech and Jesse announced:

"Some fellows have been over to the bank, robbed it of every dollar in the till, and tied up the cashier. If you all aren't too busy you might go over and untie him. I've got to be going. Thank you all for your kind attention."

Stunned members of the crowd could only stand dumbfounded as the outlaws doffed their hats, yelled, and kicked

*Allan Pinkerton, in later years.*

their mounts into a gallop back to Missouri some thirty miles south.

In Chicago, Robert Pinkerton told his father, "We must smash this gang if it is the last thing we do."

But it was not to be easy. Considered northerners, and worse, Yankees, Pinkerton agents got little help from Missouri residents. Jesse was a hero. The Pinkertons also had no accurate descriptions or photographs of James Gang members.

In an all-out effort to stop the James boys, Allan Pinkerton finally opened a branch office in Kansas City.

As time passed, Jesse and his gang became aware of the Pinkertons but he was not much concerned about them. The James boys robbed a train near Adair, Iowa in 1873, adding a new dimension to their criminal activities. And at Gads Hill (Wayne County), Missouri, late on January 31, 1874, Jesse and four friends captured a railroad station, switched a train onto a siding, snatched $22,000 and asked passengers, "Where is Mr. Pinkerton?"

Fearing the newspaper wouldn't get the story right, Jesse wrote his own news release and left it with the conductor, saying, "We like to do things in style."

---

### The Most Daring Robbery On Record

The southbound train on the Iron Mountain railroad was boarded here this evening by five heavily armed men and robbed of ____ dollars. The robbers arrived at the station a few minutes before the arrival of the train and arrested the station agent and put him under guard, then threw the train on the switch. The robbers were all large men, none of them under six feet tall. They were all masked and started in a southerly direction after they had robbed the express. They were all mounted on fine, blooded horses. There is a hell of an excitement in this part of the country.

The note did little more than insult the newspapers and the Pinkertons. In less than two months, Pinkerton men began to close in. But Pinkerton agent John M. Whicher, just 26 years old, was slain while trying to locate near the James home at Kearney, Missouri. Whicher was tied, tortured, and shot from close up. His clothes and skin were burned by the blasts. When found the next day, part of his face was missing; hog tracks surrounded the body.

The local sheriff decided the James boys were the culprits, based on information from a ferryman who'd seen the deceased with some men. Some claim the killers were Frank and Jesse, plus Clell Miller and James Latche. The local sheriff had warned, "The old woman will kill you if the boys don't." The boys apparently did.

In west-central Missouri a few days later, posing as cattle buyers, Chicago detective Louis J. Lull, former St. Louis policeman John Boyle (alias James Wright), and former Osceola deputy sheriff Edwin

B. Daniels rode along Chalk Hill Road, near Roscoe, about fifty miles northwest of Springfield. Lull and Boyle had been chasing the gang since the Gads Hill robbery. It was about 2:30 in the afternoon as Lull told the story:

"E.B. Daniels and myself were riding along the road from Roscoe to Chalk Level, which road runs past the house of one Theodore Snuffer, and about three from the town of Roscoe and in St. Clair County, Missouri.

"Daniels and myself were riding side by side, and Wright a short distance ahead of us; some noise behind us attracted our attention, and we looked back and saw two men on horseback coming toward us, and one was armed with a double barrel shot-gun, the other with revolvers; don't know if the other had a shot-gun or not; the one had the shot-gun cocked, both barrels, and ordered us to halt; Wright drew his pistol and put spurs to his horse and rode off; they ordered him to halt, and shot at him and shot off his hat, but he kept on riding. Daniels and myself stopped, standing across the road on our horses. They rode up to us, and ordered us to take off our pistols and drop them in the road, the one with the gun covering me all the time with the gun. We dropped our pistols on the ground and one of the men told the other to follow Wright and bring him back, but he refused to. I reached my hand behind me and drew a No. 2 Smith & Wesson pistol and cocked it and fired at the one on horseback, and my horse frightened at the report of the pistol turned to run and I heard two shots and my left arm fell, and then I had no control over my horse, and he jumped into the brushes and the trees checked his speed, and I tried to get hold of the rein with my right hand, to bring him into the road; one of the men rode by me and fired two shots at me, one of which took effect in my left side, and I lost control of my horse and he turned into the brush and a small tree struck me and knocked me out of the saddle. I then got up and staggered across the road and lay down until I was found. No one else was present."

Lull's Smith & Wesson killed John Younger and lawman Daniels was shot to death by Jim Younger, one of the notorious Younger brothers. (Cole, Bob and Jim Younger continued to ride with the James Gang, finally being brought down by the irate residents of

Northfield, Minnesota just over two years later. All three spent considerable time in the Minnesota State Penitentiary at Stillwater.) Lull died of his wounds.

With Lull, Daniels, and Whicher dead at the hands of the James Gang, all within a few days, the Pinkertons sought a method to trap the killers. But the Youngers had slipped away to Dallas, Texas and the James's left Missouri too.

Jesse returned in April to marry Zee Mimms, then left for Texas. Frank and Annie Ralston were married in June. Back in Missouri Pinkerton Agent Jack Ladd got work on the Dan Askew farm next to the Jameses' mother's farm near Kearney.

The boys' mother, Zerelda Cole, was by this time married for the third time. After the Reverend Mr. James passed on, she married Benjamin Simms. Simms, after just a few months of marriage, was killed accidently and in 1856 she married Dr. Reuben Samuel and they added four children to Zerelda's clan.

In January 1875, Agent Ladd reported that the James boys were at the farm! From his hotel in Kansas City, William Pinkerton, Allan's son, ordered a raid. Quickly railroad agents and Pinkerton men sped by train to Kearney. (This is, of course, what happened unofficially. The Pinkertons have never admitted to leading this raid.)

That night, they surrounded the Samuel house, tossed "a small flare with an iron base, a copper top with two curved wicks" through a window, and waited for it to light the interior of the house.

Dr. Samuel used a tobacco stick to slap it into the fireplace where the device exploded. Zerelda's mangled arm had to be amputated at the elbow. Archibald Samuel, age 8, Jesse's half-brother, died that night. Dr. Samuel was burned and cut and a servant suffered serious injuries. But the Pinkerton men failed to find Frank and Jesse.

Years would pass before the Pinkertons could forget this incident. Public sentiment swung to the Jameses. The Pinkertons emerged the bad guys.

Meanwhile, the Jameses saw to it that Dan Askew, the farmer Agent Ladd worked for, paid for his betrayal. They shot him dead on his doorstep. The Pinkertons continued their efforts, harassing the neighbors and friends of the gang, but the Pinkertons did not get the

Jameses. Bob Ford executed Jesse with a .44 caliber bullet on April 3, 1882. Frank surrendered later that year to Governor Thomas Theodore Crittenden of Missouri.

Allan Pinkerton was born to William and Isabella McQueen Pinkerton on Muirhead Street in Glasgow, Scotland in 1819. He married Joan Carfrae and they sailed for America in 1842. He made barrels in Lill's Brewery in Chicago before moving in 1843 to Dundee, Illinois and settling in as the local cooper.

Within a few years, Pinkerton discovered counterfeiters near Dundee. Before long, he was deputy sheriff, then a "special agent" to the sheriff of Cook County, and subsequently, "the first detective" on the Chicago police force.

Not long after, Pinkerton hired detectives to protect railroad property. By 1852, just ten years after the Scotsman arrived in America, he created the Pinkerton National Detective Agency. Their motto: "We Never Sleep."

After the James Gang, there were plenty of outlaws to keep the Pinkertons busy in the West. Stage robbers, train robbers and bank robbers seldom let the agency rest. There was Sam Bass, the farm boy from Lawrence County, Indiana, and his friend, Henry Underwood, from neighboring Jennings County. Pinkerton agents sought them in the 1870's.

There were many others who earned a place in the Pinkerton Rogue's Gallery and received the undying attention of Pinkerton agents until such time as they were taken out of society in one fashion or another. Some of the outlaws, like the Wild Bunch were well-known. John Wesley Hardin and Old Bill Miner were sought by the Pinkertons at one time. Frank Jackson, Red Curtis, Fred Wittrock, Thomas Eskridge, Rube and Jim Burrows, Jim Brock, Edward Estelle, and Dick, Tom and Joe McCoy, among others, made the Pinkerton "wanted" list.

In the main office in Chicago, changes were taking place. Branch offices opened across the country. Allan worked harder than ever until a stroke slowed him. He went into semi-retirement only to outline several book-length stories which were handed over to ghost writers and completed as *The Molly Maguires and the Detectives*

(1877), *The Spy of the Rebellion* (1883), and *Thirty Years a Detective* (1884).

The old Scotsman suffered another stroke in 1882. He never recovered. Death came on July 1, 1884. The agency continued its crime-fighting activities under the guidance of Allan's sons, William and Robert.

With operatives like Charlie Siringo, who started with the Pinkertons in 1886, success continued for the sons. Tom ("Killing men is my specialty") Horn was a roving agent for the Pinkertons. He quit, saying, "Too tame for me," and hired out to a Wyoming cattle company. Some say he was paid up to $500 a head for dead rustlers. Horn was hanged in 1903 for the murder of a 14-year-old boy, Willie Nickel.

Allan Pinkerton began his agency with nine employees. Today, more than 33,000 employees are located throughout North America. Until 1967, a Pinkerton always headed the firm, but an "outsider" took over that year. The agency name was changed in 1965 to Pinkerton's Inc.

James D. Horan, a Pinkerton biographer, claimed that the Pinkertons, from the 1860's into the 1900s, "in every major train or bank robbery, either captured or killed the thieves and gathered the evidence that led to scores of convictions of outlaws who were imprisoned in territorial or federal jails."

While Horan may have overlooked some that got away, it is certain that Pinkerton and his agents, and later his sons, removed a considerable measure of "wild and woolly" from the West in spite of opposition from citizens whose values sometimes made lawmen outlaws and outlaws heroes.

# 15

## Black Bart, PO8

When Horace Greeley said, "Go West, young man, Go West!" many young adventurers took his word to heart. One of those young men was Charles E. Boles, a Civil War veteran who had joined Company B, 116th Illinois Volunteer Infantry at Decatur, Illinois, early in the war. He'd joined as a private and was eventually commissioned a second lieutenant, but was mustered out on June 7, 1865 as First Sergeant. (Records even list him as first lieutenant, but show the "commission canceled," probably due to the war's ending.)

Boles had, according to most, started out in England or New York, born about 1830–32. Some have him coming to Illinois, then on to California with his brother David in search of gold during the rush. David's death caused him to return to Decatur, Illinois,where he married. After serving with the 116th, he abandoned his wife and daughters in favor of a miner's life in Idaho and Montana. He wrote letters for a while, but stopped in 1871.

By the 1870's, he was living in California, usually in Los Angeles and San Francisco with occasional forays into the gold fields. And he was prosperous. One observer described him as "a gentleman who had made a fortune and was enjoying it." He was indeed a dapper-looking man. He wore a derby hat, had a diamond stick pin, and draped a heavy gold watch and chain across his vest. He carried a gilded cane. The West had been good to him. He had made his fortune in the West, but at the expense of the Wells, Fargo Company.

Boles robbed their stages. He was good at it. From 1875 to 1883, he robbed, most agree, twenty-eight or twenty-nine Wells, Fargo stages, hauling off, some say, $18,000.

It all started on a Monday, July 26, 1875, four miles east of Copperopolis, California in the High Sierras, in Calaveras County on Funk Hill.

There was a steep incline up the hill on the stage road there and John Shine was clucking and coaxing the tired, lathered team up the grade. The stage cut through a heavy woods, brush hanging close on the side of the narrow lane. Just as the team neared the top, a ghostly-looking character stepped into the road, raising a double-barreled shotgun to the ready as he called politely, "Please throw down the box!"

The voice was hollow and deep. Shine remembered it as pleasant later, but right now all he could do was stare at the figure with the shotgun. He was dressed in white, wearing a linen duster. The dirty duster nearly touched the ground. Around the feet, Shine noticed rags wrapped to hide the shoes and footprints. Over his head, the robber wore a flour sack with holes cut so that he could see.

The thief waved the shotgun to remind Shine what he wanted, the strongbox. The stage driver began fumbling with the box, trying to pick it up from the coach's front boot. Looking quickly back toward the brush along the side of the narrow road, the highwayman called menacingly, "If he dares to shoot, give him a solid volley, boys."

Shine looked up long enough to notice several guns poking through the brush. Aimed right at him! Quickly, he threw down the wooden Wells, Fargo box.

With a lathing hatchet deftly produced from inside the linen duster, the robber slashed away at the box, breaking it open. He filled his pockets and when a frightened woman passenger on the stage threw out her purse, he responded, "Madam, I do not wish your money. In that respect, I honor only the good office of Wells, Fargo."

Calmly then, he looked up at the nervous Shine and motioned for him to drive on. And the coach and team continued the slow, lazy climb up the grade to the crest as the thief disappeared into the thick, brushy wilderness of the California forest.

When Wells, Fargo personnel returned, they found that the guns Shine saw in the brush were only sticks, tied in place to look like so many guns pointing out at them. There was little in the way of evidence, not even hoofprints.

Highway robbery was not new to Wells, Fargo. They had lost their first money to highwaymen in 1855 near Shasta, California when a mule train was robbed. It became so common that they printed a special form, a "stage robbery report." Robbed drivers and agents just had to fill in the blanks to describe the particular incident. And it is possible they might not have taken this one incident so seriously, even though their motto was "Wells, Fargo never forgets." On the other hand, they had a remarkable record of nabbing thieves and getting their losses back.

But then on June 2, 1876, at Cottonwood Peak, the robber with the linen duster and flour sack, waving a vicious shotgun, held up another Wells, Fargo stage, compounding the insult.

And on the road to Duncan Mills on the Russian River, on Friday, August 3, 1877, the same duster-clad character stepped from the brush into the road. He stopped the Point Arena stage and asked for the box, opened it, and told the driver to drive on, just as he'd done before. But this time, he added a new touch. When agents returned to the scene of the holdup they found the money box and inside was a poem:

*I've labored long and hard for bread,*
*for honor and for riches*
*But on my corns too long you've tred,*
*You fine haired Sons of Bitches,*
*    Black Bart*
*    the PO8*

So there it was. This unusual, hard-to-catch, phantom highwayman had a name. Black Bart, the Poet. It was a name that caused the vivid imaginations of newspapermen across the country to flare into prolific visions of everything from Robin Hood to the poor, downtrodden soul, getting even with the miserly Wells, Fargo money mongers. It was the thing of which newspapermen feasted — and grew wealthy.

*The dapper businessman Charles E. Boles, better known as Black Bart.*

And Wells, Fargo had stepped on some "corns" over the twenty-five years of its existence. The company virtually eliminated all of their competition the first fifteen years they were in business. (They even had the U.S. Post Office on the run at one time, causing them to reduce mail prices. Wells, Fargo's green mail boxes were all over California.) Henry Wells and William G. Fargo were absentee owners, which did not set so well with some. And their profits were so good that dividends paid to their stockholders ran as high as 22 percent a year.

As for Black Bart—some now called him the "poet laureate of road agents," his poetry did not come often, but it was enough to inspire the dime novelists of the day to great things. Over the next seven years he left behind occasional poetry and frequent smashed Wells, Fargo boxes.

Black Bart's next outing took him to another steep grade, this time between Quincy and Oroville, California. It was late July 1878. As he had done before, Black Bart stepped from the brush in front of the stage as the nearly-jaded horses crawled up the hill. As before, he was dressed the same, his feet wrapped, his body and head covered by the linen duster and flour sack. He left another note:

*Here I lay me down to sleep*
*To wait the coming morrow,*
*Perhaps success, perhaps defeat*
*And everlasting sorrow,*
*Yet come what will, I'll try it once,*
*My conditions can't be worse,*
*And if there's money in that box,*
*'Tis munney in my purse.*

And he "worked" again a couple days later and then again in October, hitting two stages within twenty-four hours. The next year, 1879, Black Bart struck three stages; four in 1880; and five each in 1881 and 1882. Always it was the same. No hoofprints. Sometimes the holdups happened within a day of each other, sometimes months would pass. Always the wicked shotgun stared the driver down. But never was the shotgun fired.

California Governor William Irwin ($300), Wells, Fargo ($300) and the U.S. government ($200) put up a reward. And gradually, Black Bart collected huge sums from them. Even more painful was the bad reputation he gave Wells, Fargo for not being able to stop this man who took money in their safekeeping from them at will. The fact that he usually robbed the U.S. Mail disturbed quite a number of folks too.

There were several lawmen working on the case from time to time. One was Sheriff Ben Thorn of Calaveras county, California. Thorn was born in New York, moved to Illinois when quite young, and taught school in Plattville, Kendall County, Illinois, beginning at age sixteen before moving on to California politics.

And there was ex-Sheriff Harry N. Morse of Alameda County, a Wells, Fargo agent working for Wells, Fargo Chief of Detectives James B. Hume.

Hume, the former sheriff of El Dorado County, California, and a California resident since he came from Indiana in 1850, was one of the pioneers of scientific detection in the United States. He was forty-six when he joined Wells, Fargo in 1873. He used his head instead of his gun to fight crime in the West. His methods worked. He was Wells, Fargo's detective chief until 1904, the year of his death.

After Black Bart robbed a stage, Hume and his detectives traveled to the area of the crime and began searching for clues, interviewing people in the surrounding countryside, trying always to come up with some sort of composite of this "poet" who was making a fool of Wells, Fargo.

As the crimes became more prevalent, Hume's job became easier. The folks he interviewed usually remembered a "magnificently mustachioed" man with gray hair. The man was a joy to dine with, a good storyteller. Most said he looked like an itinerant laborer with rough clothing, and wore boots worn and slit to relieve pressure on his corns. Others thought maybe he was a preacher. He usually wore a derby and carried a blanket roll across his shoulder. He was erect, "spare," about 40 or 50 years old, and stood about five feet eight inches tall. And he walked everywhere "at a brisk pace." Hume found that he always managed to get at least twelve miles from a robbery overnight. (On one occasion, trackers followed him for sixty miles before losing the trail in the California wilderness.)

Saturday, November 3, 1883 was the date of the break for which Hume and Wells, Fargo Company had been waiting. The Nevada Stage Company's coach on the Sonora to Milton line was being driven by Reason E. McConnell that day. At Reynolds Ferry, McConnell picked up Grandma Rolleri's son Jimmy to keep him company. The young man wanted to go hunting. As McConnell neared Copperopolis, the 19-year-old Rolleri who rode the driver's box with him, asked to be let off at the base of the steep grade coming up. Rolleri said he'd hunt the woods around the base for game and then rejoin the stage on the other side of the hill. Besides, Rolleri would lighten the load the team could have to lug up the grade. So Rolleri took his Henry rifle and waved McConnell on.

*A facsimile of the writing of Black Bart, PO8.*

McConnell clucked the team forward as Rolleri stepped into the brush that bordered the road. Near the top of the grade, Black Bart stepped from the bushes, the terrible, double-barreled shotgun raised, both hammers thumbed back, and called out to McConnell, "Who was that man—the one who got off down below?"

McConnell explained that the boy was only hunting. Out hunting stray cattle, he told Black Bart.

His mind back on his business, Black Bart ordered, "Get down from your seat. I've got to unfasten that box of yours." The Wells, Fargo box was bolted to the floor of the front boot. The team halted nervously, clouding the cool autumn air with the hot breath from their nostrils.

McConnell, breathing heavily now, said the brakes were too weak. The coach'd roll down the grade.

"The stage can't roll if you put rocks behind the wheels," Black Bart snapped. "Go ahead and do it."

"Why don't you?" McConnell replied.

Black Bart, dismayed at this man, got rocks from the side of the road, chocked the wheels and growled, "Now get down and unhitch your horses. Run then up the road a ways. I'll be busy getting that box loose."

McConnell stepped down and began unhitching the team. With all the lines clear, he slapped the team with the reins, clucking them off up the hill and away from where Black Bart was now chopping away at the iron-strapped, wooden box.

Young Jimmy Rolleri heard what was going on and started up the hill. McConnell signaled him to circle around the stage and robber and join him near the top. When Rolleri got there, McConnell took the Henry and jerked off a shot at Black Bart. Again, he blasted away. Both shots missed, whining and thwacking into the trees. Black Bart dropped awkwardly to the ground and ran off toward the brush.

In the meantime, Jimmy Rolleri took back his rifle from McConnell and said, "Here, let me shoot. I'll get him and I won't kill him either."

Rolleri jerked off a shot, Black Bart stumbled, apparently hit, but continued moving, disappearing into the brush.

Rolleri and McConnell stood gasping, wondering if they had hit him. Finally they decided to search the brush for the body. They sneaked slowly, cautiously through the low, autumn-stripped bushes. Now and then, they stopped, hushing each other. They looked around. Nothing!

Not long after, officials were out from Copperopolis searching for clues. They were joined by James Hume and Jonathan Thacker of Wells, Fargo. And before long, they found a derby hat. And there were two paper bags from Angels Camp containing crackers and sugar, and a leather case for binoculars. Over there was a magnifying glass and a razor. Later, they found two flour sacks, three dirty linen cuffs, and a handkerchief knotted with buckshot in it.

Law enforcement officials began asking throughout the area, wondering if anyone noticed anything suspicious. Sure enough, several described a graying, whiskered man who, according to Hume, fit the Wells, Fargo description of the PO8.

But the real break was on the handkerchief they'd found at the robbery site. On the handkerchief lawmen discovered a faint laundry mark—F.X.O.7. It was the clue that a thinking man, a super sleuth like James Hume needed. Six months earlier, Hume'd hired an ex-sheriff named Henry Nicholson Morse to concentrate on the Black Bart case. Hume gave Morse the handkerchief. Morse looked at it and smiled, "The first worthwhile clue we've uncovered yet."

And over the next several days, Morse checked over 90 laundries for the tell-tale mark's owner. In San Francisco a few days later, agent Harry Morse found a launderer at 113 Stevenson Street. It was Ferguson & Bigg's California Laundry and the mark was from their agency at Thomas C. Ware's tobacco shop, at 316 Post Street. Ware's records showed Charles E. Bolton as the owner. Ware said he was a mining man and resided at the Webb House at 37 Second Street.

Bolton spent much of his time in San Francisco, leaving only to inspect his mines, usually during the summer months. He read good books, wore stylish clothes, and lived in the best of hotels. Bolton couldn't be the one, the bandit.

Wells, Fargo agent Morse said later that when he saw Bolton for the first time, he was "elegantly dressed, carrying a little cane. He wore a natty little derby hat, a diamond pin, a large diamond ring on his little finger and heavy gold watch and chain. He was about five feet eight inches in height, straight as an arrow, broad-shouldered with deep sunken bright blue eyes, high cheekbones and a large handsome gray mustache."

It was hard to believe him a thief. Morse added, "He looked anything but a robber." Morse wanted to be sure he had the right man. He got Bolton to go to Hume's office and they accompanied him to his hotel and searched his belongings. There they found more clues: another handkerchief, clothing like that worn in a holdup, handwriting like Black Bart's, and a note from his wife identifying him as Charles E. Boles. They arrested him.

The investigation continued smoothly and Charles E. Boles, alias Bolton and Coulton, finally confessed several days later. It was determined that he'd never loaded the shotgun in any of the robberies. Why the name "Black Bart?" He'd read it in "The Case of Summer-field," an 1871 story that had appeared in the Sacramento *Union*. All the time, however, he insisted his name was Bolton.

One of the many stories that swelled up around this Old West mystery man said that he made a deal with Wells, Fargo, returning some of the money he'd stolen over the years. And since no one was hurt, the "deal" allowed him to plead guilty to one count of armed robbery and be sentenced to only six years in prison.

Justice was swifter in California in the 1880's, and on November 21, just 18 days after he had performed his last holdup, Boles reported to San Quentin. He was given the No. 11046 and in the four years and two months that followed, was a model prisoner.

On January 21, 1888, Boles was released. He was very popular with the newsmen again, all of them after the true story. Unfortunately, the true story was never quite as romantic as they preferred.

No one really seems to know what happened to the elusive bandit. Nevada and Montana are mentioned sometimes as places he went to re-seek his fortune. At least one account has him dying in 1917 in New York. It is reasonably certain that the wife of C.E. Boles, Mary Boles, lived at 117 Market Street in Hannibal, Missouri, as late as the 1890's.

And if he committed any other crimes he was never found out. He did tell a newsman once that his criminal career was over. The newsman asked if he would continue writing poetry. Black Bart, a gleam in his eye, admonished the reporter, "Young man, didn't you just hear me say I will commit no more crimes?"

Today, in San Andreas, California, at the corner of Main and St. Charles, stands a monument to the legend of Black Bart.

# 16      Old Bill Miner

The big steam locomotive, a metal one-eyed monster, stood halted in the forest. The big yellow light on the front of the steam engine stared down the tracks, tall straight Georgia pine trees on either side of the shining rails. The frightened fireman and engineer glowed red in the flickering light of the firebox. Nervously, the great iron and steel locomotive breathed smoke and steam, metallic huffing punctuated regularly by a hissing sound.

Just there, bathed in pale light, an old man stood, his face masked, a Baden-Powell style hat nearly hiding his clear blue eyes, his feet spread. The scene was not unlike countless others, the man's big, gnarled fist full of six-gun, the eyes glistening in the glow of the open firebox door. It was winter and just the sight of the steam seemed to warm his arthritic bones. The old train robber stepped closer to the heat and called out, "Hands up!"

It was mid-February 1911 and Old Bill Miner, after perhaps dozens of stage and train robberies, was pulling his last job. He'd come a half century and across an entire continent to this last holdup. In all his years, he'd never killed a man.

The scrawny kid from the hills of Kentucky, some say around Bowling Green, may have been born Bill Morgan or MacDonald. Various sources claim he was born in different years between 1842 and 1853, although most feel December, 1843 is about right. From a large family, Bill had sisters and at least one brother. According to most, young Bill left home in 1860 and headed west, first to Texas, then New Mexico, and finally to California.

He was honest in the beginning, working on California ranches and in mining towns as a bullwhacker, cowboy, and muleskinner. Then in 1863, while at San Diego, he got a chance at some big money. Colonel

George Wright, commanding the Union Department of the Pacific, offered a hundred dollars for a volunteer to ride to the Gila River to warn of hostile Apaches. Bill, a slender young man with the body of a jockey, said he'd go. Mounted on a fast horse and with Colonel Wright's "Godspeed!" ringing in his ears, he set out over the rolling hills east of San Diego.

The trip east was uneventful and he returned safely to collect his $100. He'd carried a few letters on the trip and decided that a postal service between San Diego and the Gila River might be a way to make a quick buck. But despite good business, Miner was soon in debt. Some claim the most valuable thing this taught him was the pattern of gold shipments and methods and routes used. But he apparently stuck to honest jobs over the next half-dozen years. Then in 1869, he robbed his first stagecoach. And over the next forty-five years he would rob others. He would also spend over thirty years in prisons in California, Canada, and Georgia. And he would become "Old Bill" Miner.

Bill was up north in California when he fell in with (some say) three hard men and picked $75,000 off the Sonora stage. Miner got the small share, but soon became the leader of his own group because he knew the routes. But it wasn't long until he was arrested and on April 3, 1866 he went on trial in San Joaquin County Court, charged with grand larceny. The judge said: "Three years at San Quentin!" On April 5, 1866 he became prisoner #3248. Then on June 6, he was tried in Placer County at Auburn for larceny. "Five years!" this judge said. At San Quentin, his new number was 3313. On July 12, 1870, they released him. He began robbing Calaveras County stages and was back in San Quentin by June 28, 1871 – #4902. San Andreas County tried him on February 9, 1872. On March 30, he got #5206 at San Quentin. He escaped May 7, 1874, was recaptured, flogged, and thrown in the dungeon. On July 14, 1880, he was released. Bill was a personable sort: Pinkerton's National Detective Agency called him "the Gentleman Bandit." Some say he was released for good behavior. One San Quentin warden described him as a "religious and gentlemanly fellow."

Bill worked in New Mexico and became popular for his fiddle-playing when he went north to Denver in late fall, 1880. Colorado seemed a good place to start anew and Bill did. With an outlaw that called himself Bill LeRoy, Miner began plying his trade anew. One night in December 1880, LeRoy and Miner took $3,600 in gold dust and coins from the Del Norte stage. The sheriff of Rio Grande County and a posse got after them. LeRoy and Miner split up. Bill took the loot, and it was a good thing because Leroy and his brother were caught by the Del Norte law and hanged by a lynch mob—after a jury found them guilty, of course. That was May 1881. (They are buried in lot 45A at Del Norte.)

Displeased with Colorado, according to most sources, Bill headed for Chicago. The Pinkertons had a profound interest in Miner by now. Tracing his movements in the Midwest led the Pinkertons to find that "he purchased an outfit of fashionable clothing," and in a few days went to Onondaga, Michigan (south of Lansing), under the name of W.A. Morgan, "a wealthy man from California." Some say he became engaged, but when his money ran out, he too left the area, apparently unannounced.

With a new friend, Stanton T. Jones of Chillicothe, Ohio, he returned to Colorado. Jones and Miner robbed a Del Norte stage near South Fork of a few hundred dollars in March 1881 and drew more posse than they'd bargained for. Several days passed with Jones and Miner in and out of gullies, ravines and canyons. All the time, when a posse led by Sheriff Lew Armstrong drew near, Bill laid down a hail of gunfire. Finally, they were caught and Jones and Miner were tied up. Miner used a concealed handgun to force a lone guard to untie them and they lit out with the posse after them again. When the posse nearly had them, Miner shot Armstrong in the arm and disabled two deputies, allowing him and Jones to escape to Arizona.

California seemed a good idea again, so Bill struck out for California southwest of Sonora in the fall of 1881. He was using the alias William Anderson and was sick. Stanton Jones nursed him back to health. He rode north after healing and became acquainted with James Connor, Bill Miller and James Crum. He and Jimmy Crum robbed the Sonora-Milton stage on November 7, 1881, getting away with $3,750. All headed for San Francisco, except for Miller who went to his ranch. Miner erred in writing a girl from Angel's Camp. She

*Old Bill Miner as he appeared in his latter years.*

promptly contacted a Wells Fargo detective named Aull—their chief investigator. Aull was to catch him when he returned from San Francisco. Miner, perhaps tipped off, went to Miller's ranch instead. Jimmy Crum went along.

Aull, not to be thwarted, came to the ranch and arrested Crum as Miner and Miller rode out in the opposite direction. A short time later, Aull and cohorts caught up with Miner and Miller and after a couple shootouts, were able to capture them. San Quentin hadn't changed much when Miner entered again on December 21, 1881. This time, he was to serve 25 years and his number was #10191.

For four years, Miner was a model prisoner, but then escaped only to be recaptured a short time later. Unfortunately, he also forfeited 51 months of good behavior time toward parole. He did not see the outside of the prison again until his release on June 17, 1902. He had served nineteen and one-half years this time. And even that was a reduction in sentence. For some time his sister, Mrs. M.J. Wellman, had been working for his release. Other circumstances that got him out early involved the efforts of him and another inmate named Jack Hayes in putting out a fire in the main shop building of the prison.

Monday, June 17, 1901, was the big day for Bill this time, only now he was indeed "Old Bill." Most figured his life of crime was done. After all, there were hardly any stages left. They considered him too old for the holdups and the daring escapes that often marked his career of crime.

Bill somehow didn't see himself that way though. The twinkle had not left his eye. He still had the winning, personable smile. Besides, there were always trains.

Miner adopted the alias of Bill Morgan and went north to western Skagit County in Washington. In Whatcom, he had a married sister named Jenny. Another sister lived at Samish Flats. But just a few weeks later, he teamed up with a young man, probably Gary Harshman, and another named Charles Hoehn. This time, they planned a train robbery, Old Bill's first.

On Wednesday, September 23, 1903, the familiar "Hands up!" rang out at Mile Post 21 near Corbett, just east of Portland, Oregon as Bill and Gary Harshman stepped down out of the tender and halted the Oregon Railroad and Navigation Company passenger train. Charles Hoehn waited there with a light and a sack. Hoehn fired a few shots at the windows to reseat the passengers and Miner took the engineer and fireman along and prepared to dynamite the baggage car. Actually, the loot was in the express car and unguarded. The agent in the baggage car opened fire with a shotgun, hitting Harshman and the engineer. Harshman was caught the next day. His wound was severe. Under questioning, he identified the others. Hoehn was captured some time later. He was sentenced to ten years; Harshman got twelve.

Somehow Miner escaped, ending up on a small farm near Princeton in British Columbia, Canada. He used the alias George Edwards and was joined later on by Jack Budd, whom most think was his brother.

In Princeton he got to know Thomas William "Shorty" Dunn. They became hunting partners and on one trip in 1904, just west of Misson Junction, British Columbia, Old Bill and Shorty bagged a train, the first train robbery in Canadian history. Their prey was a Canadian

Pacific Railway's Transcontinental Express. And it was a foggy September 10.

Between 9:30 and 10 p.m., Old Bill, Shorty, and another outlaw climbed down over the tender. Old Bill announced: "Hands up!" The engineer stopped Engine 440 at Silverdale Crossing. Bill and the others then disconnected the engine and express car from the passenger cars and continued on toward the village of Whonock. From the express car, they took $1,000 in currency, two packages of gold dust worth several thousand, and $50,000 in United States bonds.

Miner told the engineer to return to the train. In a soft drawl, Old Bill politely bade the trainman, "Good evening," then reminded him to be careful in the fog. All stops were let out to catch the outlaws. The Pinkertons were contacted. The robber was obviously American. James E. Dye, in charge of the Seattle office, got the information on the Canadian robbery, compared that to the Portland job and decided they may have been conducted by the same man. And Dye decided it had to be Bill Miner.

The reward went to $12,500 for the Mission Junction robbers and several groups began looking. All sorts of leads were followed up, but no one looked on the little town of Princeton where Miner and Dunn had settled into their former routine. Thomas "Shorty" Dunn, Rufe Hammel, and Louis Colquhoun were along on this job. The loot (some claim $10,000, others say $7,000 gold and $200,000 bonds and bills) bought him the "wealthy man from California" image he loved and let him lay low for nearly two years. Some say Bill lived at Tulameen, British Columbia. Others place him at Merritt, posing as George Edwards, rancher and livestock dealer. (One researcher says Bill and Dunn did not lay low, but took $30,000 off a train near Seattle, Washington in November 1905.)

In the meantime, Canada did not take kindly to this new tourist, their first train robber. The Canadian Pacific Railroad, the Canadian government, and the Province of British Columbia posted a $20,000 reward for Old Bill.

By May 1906, Bill needed another payday. Shorty Dunn and ex-schoolteacher Louis Colquhoun were along. Near midnight on May 8, just after the Canadian Pacific's Imperial Limited had stopped at

Ducks, Bill and Shorty came down out of the tender and halted the train. They disconnected the engine, tender and the baggage car and went ahead toward Kamloops. Unfortunately, the baggage car didn't have the loot, so they fled, disappointed, into the wild Canadian forest.

Word of the attempt jumped the reward to $20,000 and spurred the Mounted Police into action. William Fernie, the chief constable in the area, acted quickly, sending out Indian guides to track the outlaws. Calgary sent out a detachment of Mounted Police. And Miner, Dunn and Colquhoun battled the heavy rain and cool weather. On foot in the rugged country, it was just a matter of time until they were caught. Six days after the holdup and sixty miles from the holdup site, an Indian guide found three men huddled around a wet fire near the west end of Douglas Lake. It was Bill, Shorty and Colquhoun. The guide returned shortly with the Mounties. Miner and Colquhoun were captured unhurt, but Dunn took a .45 slug in the leg.

Taken to Kamloops, a photographer, a Miss M. Spencer took pictures and the trial began May 28 but ended in a hung jury. A new trial, much to the chagrin of locals who considered Bill a hero of sorts, ended in Dunn and Miner being sentenced to life. Colquhoun got 25 years. (Some claim Old Bill told the judge, politely of course, "No jail can hold me, sir.") And just in case, William Pinkerton contacted the Mounties, asking for a picture of Miner. He wanted to send Bill's photo to agents everywhere, probably anticipating Old Bill's next move. The Pinkerton's described him at the time as "Age 64 (1906), 5'8-1/2" Height, 138 lbs. Weight."

On June 3, under heavy guard, Miner, Dunn and Colquhoun headed by train for New Westminster Prison. The curious watched the mannerly Miner wave goodbye. Women cried, children waved to their friend as the train chugged out of the station. The train was greeted at every stop by crowds, all anxious to glimpse the famous Bill Miner, trainrobber.

In prison, Miner became friendly with deputy warden Bourke's daughter, Katherine. She loaned him books about religion, and quietly Miner plotted his next departure date. It came on August 8, 1907, when he and Walter Woods, John McCluskey and John Clarke escaped. (Some say they crawled out through a 35-foot tunnel under the outer wall that surrounded the brickyard at New Westminster Prison where he'd worked all day.) They separated shortly and Miner made good his escape. Canadian authorities were outraged. Even the Canadian House of Commons became upset over all this. Still he eluded detection. Where was he?

No one seems to know, although he was probably in the United States. He claimed from time to time that he went to Europe, but there is no documentation of this. Australia, England and Turkey were all included in these versions. At least, that's the story he told a friendly detective. He claimed London was his first stop. Then he toured Europe. The detective wondered if he'd robbed any trains there. Bill smiled, his eyes twinkling. No, but he admitted he'd considered it more than once. He did say he was in cahoots with a Turk and that together they'd conducted a profitable slave trade.

Africa was Bill's next stop and he claimed he sized up a diamond train, but there were too many guards. Not long after, he sailed to Rio de Janeiro and before long, back to the United States.

From August 1907 to 1910, no one seems to know Bill's whereabouts for certain, although one report has him taking $12,000 from a Portland, Oregon bank.

For Old Bill, these were rough times. It seemed someone was always right behind him, hounding his every move. One account has him working in Pennsylvania in a sawmill, using the name George Anderson. He moved on to Virginia to another sawmill, then to Lula, Georgia.

And so it was in mid-February 1911, that Bill, Charles Hunter, and George Handford invaded Dixie, holding up a Southern Railway Express near White Sulphur Springs in Meriwether County in a Georgia pine woods. Old Bill was tanned and his hair was snow-white. The big white mustache still sagged and moved with that friendly, reassuring smile; the clear, blue eyes still had that gleam, but by now the old, big pistol shook in his rheumy hand, often wobbly, seemingly out of control. Still, he could shoot. And he could still ride.

They blew the baggage car and took $2,000, but had no luck with the safe. After bidding the train crew goodnight, the robbers rode out.

There are different versions of what happened next. One story has the three splitting, Miner bound for Gainesville, Handford and Hunter headed north. This story has Old Bill picked up for vagrancy and held there in the county jail until identified by a Pinkerton agent.

What ever the circumstances, times were changing. Crime fighters were organized, smarter, more sophisticated. Transportation and communication were leaving the horse-and-buggy days far behind. Old ways gave way to new. After all, it was the Twentieth Century!

A second version says that when word got to Atlanta that a train robbery had occurred, Henry W. Minster got the word. Minster, a Pinkerton operative, grabbed a train for Gainesville to interview the train crew. Then he used a telephone to contact local sheriffs and sheriffs along the Appalachian Mountains all the way to Pennsylvania.

Within hours, the sheriff of Lumpkin County in north-central Georgia telephoned Minster to say he'd had a tip. There were strange campers in his county. It was a Twentieth Century break for law enforcement.

This story has Minster, the county sheriff, and a posse going in at night. As they drew near the circle of light created by Old Bill's fire, Miner, groggy with sleep, yelled, "Rouse, boys, the law is on us." He came up on his knees and punctuated the alarm with rifle fire, snapping off shots into the brush as fast as he could.

The posse returned the fire and mowed down two of the gang. And then as quickly as it started, Miner threw his gun away and his hands up. The cool fire danced, flickering shadows bouncing off leafless brush, gunsmoke hanging in layers, clouding the scene. Miner called out, dejected, yet almost relieved, "Well, I guess you got me, boys."

Minster snapped handcuffs on him and asked, "What's your name?"

"William Morgan," Bill lied, that old gleam in his eye.

Minster studied his face in the dim light, then said, "You look familiar to me."

Bill smiled broadly and shrugged.

Later Minster sent a picture of Miner to the Chicago office. William Pinkerton responded by telegram: "Morgan is Bill Miner, California's train and stage robber. Alias William Morgan, George

Anderson, Sam Anderson, California Billy, Old Bill, Budd and G.W. Edwards. Escaped from New Westminster Penitentiary, Victoria, British Columbia."

Minster showed Bill the wire and the old man flashed a smile, "That's me."

On March 11, 1911, Miner, George Handford and Charles Hunter were sentenced. Miner asked to be sent back to a Canadian prison. William Pinkerton thought that a good idea. But the judge in Gainesville decided that Miner wasn't up to it physically, so he sent him to the Newton County chain gang. He was transferred to the Georgia State Penitentiary at Milledgeville not long after. This time the sentence was life. Really.

Bill tended a garden when he wasn't escaping. On October 21, 1911, he and Tom Moore escaped and stayed out for two and one-half weeks. They made it to St. Clair, Georgia, hid in a boxcar, but after a shootout left Moore dead, Miner surrendered. He was in bad shape, but not beaten. Prison officials thought they'd best put him in a ball and chain this time.

On June 29, 1912, he sawed through the chains, and the bars on his cell and with two friends, escaped again! They made it through a swamp to a river, got a boat and headed downriver. The boat turned over, one of the men was drowned and Bill separated from the other. He waded through several miles of swamp, pushing murky, waist-deep water in front of him. Finally, the posse and dogs caught him. Old Bill, weary, his face worn and creased, mustered a hint of a smile and said pitifully, "I guess I'm getting too old for this sort of thing."

Back in prison, he spent most of the rest of his days in a hospital. A guard found him dead on September 2, 1913, of a gastric ulcer. He died where he'd spent nearly half of his life—in prison.

Old Bill was given a funeral by the townsfolk of Milledgeville and interred in the Milledgeville Cemetery. During the 1960s, a stone was placed on his grave. According to one source, the gravestone refers to Miner as "the last of the famous Western Bandits."

# Bibliography

Alfeld, Philip J. "Major Reno and His Family in Illinois." *The English Westerner's Brand Book,* 13 (July 1971): 4–6.

Ambrose, Stephen E. *Crazy Horse and Custer.* Garden City, NY: Doubleday & Company, Inc., 1975.

Anderson, Frank W. *Bill Miner: Stagecoach and Train Robber.* Surrey, B.C.: Frontier Books, 1982.

Andrist, Ralph K. *The Long Death: the Last Days of the Plains Indians.* New York, NY: The Macmillan Company, 1964.

Bartholomew, Ed. *Wyatt Earp: The Man and the Myth.* Toyahvale, TX: Frontier Book Co., 1964.

– – –. *Wyatt Earp: The Untold Story.* Toyahvale, TX: Frontier Book Co., 1963.

Boatner, Mark Mayo. *The Civil War Dictionary.* New York, NY: David McKay Company, Inc., 1967.

Brady, Cyrus Townsend. *Indian Fights and Fighters.* Lincoln, NE: University of Nebraska Press, 1971.

Brininstool, E.A. *A Trooper With Custer.* Columbus, OH: 1926.

– – –. "Charley Reynolds – Hunter and Scout." *North Dakota Historical Quarterly,* 7 (1932–33).

Brown, Dee Alexander. *Bury My Heart At Wounded Knee.* New York, NY: Holt, Rinehart & Winston, 1970.

— — —. *The Fetterman Massacre.* Lincoln, NE: University of Nebraska Press, 1971.

— — —. *The Gentle Tamers: Women of the Old Wild West.* Lincoln, NE: University of Nebraska Press, 1970.

— — —. *Showdown at Little Big Horn.* New York, NY: G.P. Putnam's Sons, Inc., 1964.

— — —. *The Westerners.* New York, NY: Holt, Rinehart & Winston, 1974.

— — —. *The Year of the Century: 1876.* New York, NY: Charles Scribner's Sons, 1966.

Brown, Jesse and Williard, A.M. *The Black Hills Trails.* Rapid City, SD: Rapid City Journal Company, 1924.

Bryan, Jerry. "An Illnois Gold Hunter in the Black Hills." (Diary, March 13—August 20, 1876). Pamphlet Series No. 2, Illinois State Historical Society, Springfield, IL, 1960.

Connell, Evan S. *Son of the Morning Star.* San Francisco, CA: North Point Press, 1984.

Connelley, William E. *Wild Bill and His Era.* New York, NY: The Press of Pioneers, 1933.

Coons, Frederica. *The Trail to Oregon.* Portland, OR: Binfords & Mort, 1954.

Dary, David A. *The Buffalo Book.* New York, NY: Avon Books, 1974.

DeArment, Robert K. *Bat Masterson: The Man and the Legend.* Norman, OK: University of Oklahoma Press, 1979.

– – –. *Knights of the Green Cloth: The Saga of the Frontier Gamblers.* Norman: University of Oklahoma Press, 1982.

Dillon, Richard. *Wells, Fargo Detective: The Biography of James B. Hume.* New York, NY: Coward-McCann, Inc., 1969.

Eastman, Charles A. "The Story of the Little Big Horn." *Chautauqua Magazine,* Vol. 31, No. 4 (1900).

Faulk, Odie B. *Tombstone: Myth and Reality.* New York, NY: Oxford University Press, 1972.

Garland, Hamlin. *The Book of the American Indian.* New York, NY: Harper Bros., 1923.

Graham, W.A., ed. *Abstract of the Official Proceedings of the Reno Court of Inquiry.* Harrisburg, PA: The Stackpole Company, 1954.

– – –. *The Custer Myth: A Source of Custeriana.* New York, NY: Bonanza Books, 1953.

– – –. *The Story of the Little Bighorn.* New York, NY: The Century Company, 1926.

Gray, John S. "Last Rites for Lonesome Charley Reynolds." *Montana: The Magazine of Western History,* 13 (July 1963) 40– 51.

Hans, Fred M. "Diary of – –, 1879: A Visit With Sitting Bull." *South Dakota Historical Collections,* 40 (1980) 128–135.

Hanson, Joseph Mills. *The Conquest of the Missouri.* New York, Holt, Rinehart & Winston, 1946.

*Hardin (Montana) Tribune,* June 22, 1923.

Horan, James D. *The Authentic Wild West: The Outlaws.* New York, NY: Crown Publishers, Inc., 1977.

— — — and Sann, Paul. *Pictorial History of the Wild West.* New York, NY: Crown Publishers, 1954.

— — —. *The Pinkertons: The Detective Dynasty That Made History.* New York, NY: Bonanza Books, 1967.

Hunt, Frazier and Robert. *I Fought With Custer: The Story of Sergeant Charles Windolph.* New York, NY: Charles Scribner's Sons, 1954.

Kirby, Ed. "Bill Miner—The Grey Fox: He was an Outlaw for Nearly Fifty Years!" *Quarterly of the National Association and Center for Outlaw and Lawman History.* Vol. X, No. 1, Summer 1985.

Larpenteur, Charles. *Forty Years a Fur Trader.* Chicago, IL: R.R. Donnelley & Sons Co., 1941.

Libby, O.G. "Arikara Narrative of the Campaign Against the Hostile Dakotas, June, 1876." *North Dakota Historical Collections,* 6 (1920).

McCreight, M.I. *Chief Flying Hawk's Tales.* New York, NY: Alliance Press, 1936.

Marquis, Thomas B. *Sitting Bull and Gall, the Warrior.* Hardin, Montana: Privately Printed, 1934.

— — —. *Wooden Leg: A Warrior Who Fought Custer.* Lincoln, NE: University of Nebraska Press, 1971.

Martin, Douglas D. *The Earps of Tombstone.* Tombstone, AZ: Tombstone Epitaph, 1959.

Mayer, Frank H. and Roth, Charles B. *The Last of the Buffalo Hunters.* Chicago, IL: The Swallow Press, 1972.

Miller, David Humphreys. "Echoes of the Little Bighorn." *American Heritage,* 22 (June 1971) 28–41.

Miller, Nyle H. and Snell, Joseph W. *Great Gunfighters of the Kansas Cowtowns.* Lincoln, NE: University of Nebraska Press, 1967.

Monaghan, Jay, ed. *The Book of the American West.* New York, NY: Bonanza Books, 1963.

– – –. *The Life of General George Armstrong Custer.* Boston, MA: Little, Brown and Company, 1959.

Moody, Ralph. *Stagecoach West.* New York, NY: Thomas Y. Crowell Co., 1967.

Neihardt, John G. *Black Elk Speaks.* Lincoln, NE: University of Nebraska Press, 1961.

Ness, George T. Jr. "Illinois at West Point: Her Graduates in the Civil War." *Journal of the Illinois State Historical Society,* 35, 338–346.

*New York Herald,* August 8, 1876; October 6, 1876; January 22, 1878.

*New York Times,* July 7, 1876.

O'Neill, George F. "A Letter: Asst. President of Pinkerton's, Inc. to Larry D. Underwood," January 24, 1984.

Pawley, Eugene. "He Out-robbed Jesse James." *Old West,* 28 (Winter 1964) 28–29, 48.

Remsburg, John E. and George J. *Charley Reynolds.* Kansas City, MO: H.M. Sender, 1931.

Reynolds, Charles and Alexander Brown. "Combined Journal, 1876." Minnesota Historical Society.

Rosa, Joseph G. *They Called Him Wild Bill.* Norman, OK: University of Oklahoma Press, 1964.

St. Paul, Minnesota *Pioneer Press,* May 19, 1883.

"Sitting Bull." *The Voice of Peace,* 6 (September 1879), 86.

Smith, Rex Alan. *Moon of Popping Trees.* Lincoln, NE: University of Nebraska Press, 1981.

Snell, Joseph W. "Diary of a Dodge City Buffalo Hunter, 1872–1873." *The Kansas Historical Quarterly,* 31(4), Winter 1965.

Turner, John Peter. *The North-West Mounted Police, 1873–1893.* (2 vols.) Ottawa, Ont.: King's Printer and Controller of Stationary, 1950.

Underwood, Larry D. "Comanche—The Sole Survivor." *Canada Rides.* 1974.

———. "It Didn't Happen at the O.K. Corral: The Earps." *Illinois Magazine,* December, 1977.

———. "Marcus A. Reno: An Illinoisan at the Little Big Horn." *Illinois Magazine,* November, 1979.

———. *Tatankaiyotake: Sitting Bull.* Filmstrip script. Minneapolis, MN: Life Educational Productions, 1973.

———. *Those Westering Women.* Filmstrip script. Des Moines, IA: Perfection Form Co., 1976.

Utley, Robert M. and Washburn, Wilcomb E. *The American Heritage History of the Indian Wars*. New York, NY: American Heritage Publishing Co., Inc., 1977.

Utley, Robert M. "Custer Battlefield National Monument." *National Park Service Historical Handbook*. Washington, D.C., 1969.

— — —. *Frontier Regulars: The United States Army and the Indian— 1866–1891*. New York, NY: Macmillan Publishing Co., Inc., 1973.

— — —. *The Indian Frontier of the American West: 1846–1890*. Albuquerque, NM: University of New Mexico Press, 1984.

Van Slyke, Sue C. "The Truth About the Clantons." *Quarterly of the National Association and Center for Outlaw and Lawman History,* 7 (Spring 1982) 12–16.

Vestal, Stanley. *Sitting Bull: Champion of the Sioux*. Norman, OK: University of Oklahoma Press, 1980.

# Index